THE MINDSET GUIDE
For
WINNERS

----

5 STEPS TO BECOME A CHAMPION IN YOUR LIFE

Systematically Create Abundance & Health in Your Life,
Financial Freedom, Fulfilling Career, Strong Relationships,
And Inner Peace

THE MASTER METHOD ACADEMY

with
GRANDMASTER MARCO SIES
7-TIME KICKBOXING WORLD CHAMPION

CONTENTS

In loving memory of Hector Vera, my beloved grandfather. His genuine kindness and gentle spirit touched my soul, and his presence remains a guiding light, reminding me to live with compassion and cherish every precious moment.

ACKNOWLEDGMENTS

I began writing the concepts for this book many years ago, and although it was a long journey, I enjoyed every step. The process taught me so much, and it was a wonderful and exciting experience.

I'm humbly grateful, and I would first like to acknowledge all of the great masters and teachers who came before us, leaving such valuable knowledge and wisdom through writings, stories, and experiences. I was greatly influenced and learned not only from my own experiences but through countless hours of reading and listening to the teachings of ancient and contemporary masters.

This book could not have been possible without my wife Julie. To her, with all my love, I'm grateful. Not just for this book, but for the opportunity to share each day with her and live such a wonderful life. I'm thankful for her love and unconditional constant support, combined with her guidance and incredible ability to transform my words and ideas into an organized and tangible manuscript. My gratitude is also with our children, who give us so many reasons to be thankful, for truly blessing us every day, and allowing us the opportunity to experience a life of pure happiness and joy as their parents. I'm so proud of each one of them, and I'm grateful for every moment we're able to share.

Thank you also to my friends, family, and students, who are so supportive and show such love. I feel blessed to have you in my life.

This book is based on concepts I've learned, practiced, and teach, but it wouldn't have been possible without our amazing production team. Many years ago, Richy Sharshan, my editor, turned my writings into a work of art. She masterfully presented my story, preserving my words and concepts. Goli Kaviani, with her incredible artistic creativity, took care of our photographic needs. And to the many other team members who made our publications possible--THANK YOU! We couldn't have asked for a better group of individuals to work with, and we're forever grateful for your countless hours going above and beyond, all your hard work and efforts, and most of all—your friendship and support.

Most importantly, thank YOU for reading, and inspiring me on this journey. It is a privilege and an honor, and I humbly thank you for the opportunity to share my story and the lessons I've learned with you. I hope these lessons will inspire you as well, helping you create the wonderful life you truly deserve.

With gratitude,

Grandmaster Marco Sies

INTRODUCTION

ANCIENT IDEAS FOR MODERN TIMES

The lessons in this book outline concepts I could never credit to my own invention. Most of these ideas are ancient principles that have been taught for thousands of years, and the principles are timeless and universal. The most influential people throughout history knew how to apply this wisdom, and if you look closely at their legacies, you'll no doubt recognize many of the concepts presented here in *The Mindset Guide for Winners*.

COMPILING UNIVERSAL PRINCIPLES

In here, you'll find compiled, organized, and applied to today's living, the wisdom of the great masters – Jesus, Buddha, Mohammed, Hermes Trismegistus, Lao Tzu, Socrates, Plato, and other teachers in ancient history. In addition, we've also distilled a wealth of knowledge from some of the most remarkable teachers of modern history — Albert Einstein, Napoleon Hill, Mahatma Gandhi, Mother Theresa, Jack Canfield, Tony Robbins, Ester Hicks, Stephen Covey, etc., whose universal principles have been presented in so many valuable ways to help millions of people live better and realize success.

THE MASTER METHOD – 5 STEPS TO SUCCESS, PROSPERITY AND INNER PEACE

After decades of studying ancient masters and philosophers, as well as contemporary motivators and performance coaches, I began to realize there were repeating patterns of wisdom being taught over centuries and generations of masters. I realized I was achieving my own incredible successes over and over again, and I was repeatedly using the same systematic method to reach virtually every goal I set. Not even realizing it, the process I was using had evolved from studying the collective teachings of the greatest masters of all time. So, I began to define, detail, and share the process with my students, and I called it "The Master Method" in honor of its ancient roots.

In my life, I used this 5-step "Master Method" to overcome and learn from every challenge I faced. I experienced bullying, poverty, illness, injury, and even homelessness. Still, I was able to endure, strengthen and conquer every obstacle to achieve seven world championships, build successful businesses, publish this book, improve my health, and most importantly – find the love of my life and inner peace I had been searching for since I was so young. I've also seen how this method has touched the lives of thousands of students over the years, from athletes, coaches, children, and parents, to people struggling with finances, health, relationships, and inner peace.

SUCCESS COMES WITH PRACTICE

The Mindset Guide for Winners is not a presentation of new concepts, but a new presentation of ancient and modern concepts. The 5-step process is simply presented and has empowered thousands to gain control of their own successes, to CHOOSE happiness, to give them the mindset guide to create winning habits, overcome challenges, and proactively CREATE the life they want.

Sharing my story with you allows me to let you know that I have experienced my fair share of challenges, and I know what it's like to not be where you want to be YET. But I am here to tell you that you can accomplish anything you desire, knowing you have the keys to open the beautiful gates of joy, abundance, wealth, prosperity, and success in all areas of your life.

Allow me to hand over those keys to you now and show you how to use them. Then it's up to you to reflect, decide, plan, condition, take consistent action, and start creating your winning life!

"Believe It, Achieve It!"

~ Grandmaster Marco

PROLOGUE

THE MAKING OF A CHAMPION

I t was a brutal left hook I will never forget that knocked me to the mat early in the second round of my first big fight in America. I knew at that moment I was completely outclassed. Stunned, I got back up, thinking to myself, "Even if I don't win this match, I will at least make this guy remember my name." I fought back fiercely and bravely, getting back up again and again until the referee ordered me to stay down late in the third round. And so ended the big debut of Marco "Babyface" Sies on national television.

You might have expected me to begin this book with one of my triumphant world championship victories … or perhaps a poignant moment on the memorable day I was inducted into the Karate World Hall of Fame as a Legend in Kickboxing. But I chose what some people would consider to be a disastrous failure for a good reason: to show that losing is nothing more than a big part of winning, and if you accept it as part of the process of achieving your goals, you'll become stronger and better equipped to continue toward your aspirations.

I ended up in the hospital that night, but with a conviction stronger than ever to become the fastest, smartest, and technically best fighter on the planet. I later learned I had been set up against an Olympic champion by managers who assured me I would do fine, even though I was a kickboxer who had never trained in traditional boxing. Despite losing that fight, the heart I showed in those three rounds sparked a lot of interest in the baby-faced kid from South America, opening doors that led me closer to my dream. How did I develop the drive and determination that kept me on the path to success? It's a journey that began in the busy city of Santiago, Chile, where I was born.

SMALL BOY, BIG THINKER

I grew up in humble surroundings in Santiago, a city that's gritty and tough, but enchanting in its natural beauty, set in a lush valley at the foot of the Andes Mountains. Although my family's means were meager, and I faced perhaps more than my share of troubles, I look back in appreciation to the people and experiences that shaped who I became and steered me toward my life today.

I was the oldest of three sons born to a mother and father who worked very hard to provide my brothers and me with the necessities and education every parent wishes for their child. However, as kids, we didn't feel the struggle  they must have experienced raising us, as we were just three little boys who found joy in the simplest things. We spent hours outdoors getting as dirty as possible, and we made several (unsuccessful) attempts at testing our parachuting abilities off the roof of our house. Always fascinated by nature, I remember hiding from, stalking, and eventually catching a variety of bugs, lizards, birds, and other wild creatures with my bare little hands.

 From an early age, I loved to read about the world around me, and I spent hours observing people, attempting to figure out why they behaved the way they did. At the age of eight, I read Carl Sagan's *Cosmos* and it intrigued me; were there humans on other planets? What was the cycle of life? Why are people the way they are? Why does the mind work as it does? An analytical child, I was fascinated with human psychology, fervently observing my parents, relatives, and other adults, sometimes to their annoyance.

My most comforting and peaceful memories are the wonderful times I spent fishing with my grandfather in the beauty and quiet of the trickling streams and pristine lakes high in the rugged mountains of Chile. My grandfather, whom we lovingly referred to as "Tata," not only taught me to fish, but he taught me how to live a life of true happiness and peace. To this day, I love to fish, and I find great joy and tranquility in these moments.

My Tata was the kindest, gentlest, and most humble soul I have ever known. He represented integrity, selflessness, and honor — a true gentleman. He was my ultimate role model and the type of person I would spend my life striving to become. Despite many stumbling blocks, mistakes, and bad choices I made along my journey, my Tata was always my grounding spirit and my foundation. He stood like a lighthouse guiding me to want to be a better person. He also represented a wonderful place of peace, joy, and fulfillment, and I am so grateful every day for this man's powerfully positive influence in my life.

PERSONAL STRUGGLES

Those fond recollections of childhood are the memories I choose to remember and on which I place my focus. However, growing up I also experienced difficulties and personal conflicts that I've worked very hard to overcome. Some of these struggles stemmed from negative influences and people who told me I wasn't good enough ... I was inferior ... I wasn't smart ... I was too poor, too small, too unattractive. I was told so many negative things so often, I spent many years believing these things were true, and it took me a very long time to break the negative cycle of thoughts and behaviors that resulted.

 Very small for my age, I was a dark-skinned boy living in a not-yet diversified population where light skin was admired and favored. At school, little girls told me I was ugly, and the boys bullied me relentlessly. I have stories, as so many children do, of schoolyard taunting — I remember being thrown headfirst into a trashcan and the humiliation of a group of boys chasing me, whipping me with their neckties, and making me run like a horse while they laughed. I had teachers tell me I was dirty because of my dark pigmentation, and even some of my own relatives made hurtful comments, all fueling my fears that I was unworthy, and affecting my self-image, my confidence, and my entire being. Added to that was a troubled relationship between my mother and father, who eventually divorced, and some personal traumatic experiences which contributed even more to my feelings of unworthiness and self-doubt.

Looking back on those years, knowing what I know now, I see how many of these negative childhood experiences stayed with me well into adulthood and heavily influenced the way I handled relationships, among other things. However, I now understand that these experiences later helped me build my resilience, motivation, and to identify what I *didn't* want for myself. Those experiences helped me realize how far I've come, and to truly appreciate the wonderful life I have now.

GROWING UP IN A MACHO WORLD

As many boys do, I admired my father - a police detective and former military man. He and my uncles were into the martial arts, and by the age of five or six, I already had a fascination with martial arts, and I persistently pleaded with my dad to show me moves and "train" me. I grew up wanting to be a great fighter, but no one took this undersized boy seriously - especially one who also had his head buried in philosophy books most of the time.

People told me I was weird and crazy. I had so many questions about the world around me, and I finally felt validated when I discovered the writings of the great philosophers. I began reading Darwin and consumed everything I could find on Greek philosophy. Although I attended Catholic school, I studied the teachings of various religions — Muslim, Buddhist, and even gnostic beliefs. Between the ages of 13 and 16, I wrote more than 100 essays on philosophy and psychology. Constantly studying the way people moved and behaved, I noticed, for example, the difference in the way my father interacted with his friends versus his family. I found it all fascinating.

As a teenager, I started to study philosophy and meditation seriously, and the negativity of my early childhood years began to change dramatically. I signed up for a philosophy program at one of our local schools, and I was the only youngster in a class full of adults. Not realizing it was subsidized by donations and student support, when it came time to make a contribution, a kindhearted woman in my class made a donation on my behalf when she saw I had nothing to give. Because of her generosity, I was able to continue my studies, and I feel such gratitude for her to this day.

During this time I also diligently continued my martial arts training, determined to prove the doubters wrong. At times, the subconscious thoughts and feelings from my childhood crept back, and I would find myself challenged. But now, I was equipped with the principles from ancient wisdom and teachings to help me overcome negative thoughts and feelings, proactively shift into a positive mindset, and get back on track.

LIFE CHANGES AND A NEW DETERMINATION

When I was 15, an exhibition by world champion kickboxer Bill "Superfoot" Wallace in my hometown changed the course of my life. I was awed by his power, mastery and discipline, and I decided that very night I wanted to become a world champion. I decided I WOULD become a world champion. I would train and learn and work harder than anyone else ever had and let nothing stop me from reaching my goal. Of course, when I shared my thoughts with others, they scoffed and laughed at me, but I was now even stronger in my conviction, my decision was made, and I began to make my plan.

In the summer of that same year, our father left and suddenly my mother was divorced and struggling to feed, clothe and educate three children. She had to work long hours to provide for our basic needs, so she was not in any position to help me with "luxuries" such as training to become the world champion! We didn't have the financial means for anything but basic necessities, and even that was a struggle. It was a huge obstacle, and some might have allowed it to stop them, or to put their dreams aside. However, I knew I HAD to make this work, and I would have to make it work on my own.

I began working every job I could find to earn even the smallest amount of money, knowing every little bit would help. I washed dishes, I helped people carry groceries to their cars, I swept floors, and I even walked several miles to and from school so I could save my bus money for training tuition. I was determined to accomplish my goal, and I knew every little bit would help me get closer to it.

It was difficult at times, especially when I faced trying circumstances or negative influences from others whose "advice" or discouragement could have potentially diminished my faith. However, I somehow managed to keep my mind strong and maintain my focus on what I WANTED, rather than focusing on the obstacles or the negative influences of others.

BELIEVING AND STAYING THE COURSE

Little by little, small opportunities began to fall into my path, and eventually, I was able to find work at a martial arts school cleaning floors, bathrooms, and mirrors. I never looked at these duties as beneath me, but rather as an opportunity. Because I set out to become the *best* floor/bathroom/mirror cleaner, I soon earned more responsibilities and eventually the chance to begin assisting with martial arts classes. I realized that by doing *everything* with the best effort and enthusiasm, it would open the doors to increasingly better opportunities. AND it made me feel good in the process!

This first martial arts job allowed me to train and improve my martial arts and kickboxing skills, and after a couple of years of grueling work and unrelenting training, I proudly reached the great achievement of becoming the Chilean National Champion. I was only eighteen years old, and it was an enormous accomplishment. I maintained my title for the next three years, but my eyes were still on the world title. Unfortunately, my odds of winning such a title were improbable if I remained in Chile. By age 21, I had accomplished all I could in South America, and I knew I had to go to Europe or the United States, where there were more events, more promoters, and more prospects for reaching my ultimate goal.

COMING TO AMERICA

Expressing gratitude is an important part of the process of achieving success, and my journey to the U.S. began with two incredible acts of kindness for which I will be forever grateful.

The day before I left Chile, I visited my beloved Tata to say goodbye. To this day, I feel moved to tears remembering the gift he gave me that day with such great love and devotion —$40. Although a small amount to most, it was his life's savings, put aside penny by penny into a small cardboard box he carried with him. It was his way of showing he loved and supported me. I will never forget his generous present, which was not about the money, but was a priceless gift of compassion and faith I will cherish forever in my heart, knowing he believed in me.

The other person who helped to make my quest possible was my Aunt Elizabeth, who lived in Virginia and allowed me the opportunity to stay with her my first year in the States, and she gave me my first job with her cleaning company.

And so, without looking back, I left my homeland of Chile, and I arrived in America with the $40 from my Tata, a couple of pairs of pants and shirts, some music tapes, and my martial arts uniforms. I was twenty-one years old and spoke very little English, but I was here to fulfill my dream of becoming the lightweight kickboxing champion of the world.

A NEW NICKNAME

I settled into an ambitious routine, working as a cleaner late at night, delivering newspapers in the early morning hours and still training at every opportunity. I also began to look for a promoter to represent me, but my baby face was proving to be a hindrance. No one believed I was old enough to fight! Things definitely seemed hopeless at times, and the challenges were many.

I was a naive kid whose skills in a new language weren't the strongest. The world of kickboxing is a tough business with purses going mostly to the promoters and the actual fighter taking the physical punishment for only $200 or $300 per fight at most. We would often drive all night to get to an event and go straight to the weigh-in. I would fight and we would drive straight back home because hotel accommodations weren't in the budget. While the pay was far from enough to cover any bills, I knew I was building my reputation and my name, which now included a new nickname — I was now billed as Marco "Babyface" Sies.

In those early years, I met people who promised me training, fights, and other "deals," but I didn't understand anything about contracts and was so green I assumed no one would be unethical or have bad intentions. At one point, I was convinced to travel to California with the promise of big money for just a couple of fights. I spent two months there and never got paid a dime. I returned to the East Coast with nothing — no job, no money, and no place to live.

LOSING EVERYTHING

At this low point, I found myself homeless, and I didn't know where my next meal would come from. I didn't want to burden my aunt and uncle because they had problems of their own. So, for a couple of months, I slept in my car or at one of my cleaning jobs after hours. For food, I would stand outside different grocery stores asking people for a quarter to make a phone call, and when I had just enough coins, I would buy an orange juice and a Snickers bar or a loaf of bread.

Despite these major setbacks, I was so focused on becoming a world champion, I never lost my faith. My thoughts were filled with achieving that end result and doing whatever I had to do to get there. And soon, little by little, things began to turn around. Without knowing why, I was accepting everything I experienced as part of my journey. Somehow I knew I was being led closer and closer to my destination through these tests. Now I look back on these hardships with gratitude for the lessons I learned. In hindsight, I realize each trial gave me the knowledge and tools I needed to become a kickboxing world champion. Even during the worst of times, I still truly believed I was on the path to becoming a world champion. I spent time meditating each day and my focus in those mediations was not on my current situation but on my dream of where I wanted to be.

Within a few months, I was back on my feet, and even though I had to work even harder to sustain myself, I didn't worry. I knew it was all part of the process.

I couldn't afford a boxing gym, so I did what I had to do in order to train. I found an old couch near a dumpster, took the cushions off, tied them to a tree, and that became my punching bag! I trained in the parking garage at a local mall, running up and down the stairs, I ran sprints in a local park, and I also trained in the forest and mountains nearby. I used all the creative means I could think of to continue my training every single day in hot sun, rain, or snow.

A WINNER EMERGES

Despite my first disastrous televised fight, another big fight eventually came my way, and it changed the course of my career.

I actually knocked out the hometown favorite in an impressive victory in Rochester, New York.

It was my first title in North America and I was joyously happy! The next day, I was told the president of the International Kickboxing Council, Grandmaster Keith Nesbitt, Sr., wanted to speak to me. He was impressed by my performance the night before and he was curious to know how I trained. He was shocked to hear I had no training facilities and was deeply moved by my story.

When I returned home, I found that his associates had delivered all kinds of equipment so I could train properly.

Everything I could have dreamed of to train with, he sent. To this day, I am so thankful for the wonderful gesture from this kind Grandmaster whose compassion touched me to my core and will always hold my deepest gratitude, respect, and admiration.

BEYOND MY BOYHOOD DREAMS

After that victory, many fights came, as well as a great team of trainers and supporters. And finally, in the year 2000, after twelve years of conditioning my mind and body and countless challenges, setbacks, and obstacles, the day I dreamed of for what seemed like a lifetime arrived. I was named the USKBA Super Lightweight Professional Full-Contact Kickboxing World Champion! The joy, excitement, pride, and gratitude that washed over me in that moment will stay with me always. When they announced my name, so many memories and images came flooding back to me … the moment I made my decision at age 15 to become a world champion … the emotional scene of my Tata presenting his love and faith to me … the dismay of being homeless and broke … all of the aches, pains, hard work and hope along the journey. I was finally at my destination. It was an incredible arrival, and I still think about it with excitement in my heart.

WORLD CHAMPION
GRANDMASTER MARCO SIES

M arco Sies has trained in martial arts for over four decades, including full-contact kickboxing, Muay Thai, Karate, Shotokan, Gojuryu, Kyokushin, Tae Kwon Do, Hapkido, Jiu Jitsu and professional boxing. The following time-line highlights many of his accomplishments and honors in competition, martial arts and business.

World Champion Grandmaster Marco Sies

Marco Sies has trained in martial arts for over four decades, including full-contact kickboxing, Muay Thai, Karate, Shotokan, Gojuryu, Kyokushin, Tae Kwon Do, Hapkido, Jiu Jitsu and professional boxing. The following timeline highlights many of his accomplishments and honors in competition, martial arts and business.

1992   WAKO Featherweight Chilean National Professional Kickboxing Low Kick Champion

1997   IKC Featherweight Professional Kickboxing Champion
KIKA Lightweight Professional Kickboxing Champion

2000   USKBA Super Lightweight Professional Full-Contact Kickboxing World Champion

2002   WWKF Lightweight Professional Full-Contact Kickboxing World Champion

2003   PKF Lightweight Professional Full-Contact Kickboxing World Champion

2004   WPKO Lightweight Professional Full-Contact Kickboxing World Champion

2005   KICK Super Lightweight Professional Full-Contact Kickboxing World Champion
USKBA Lightweight Professional Full-Contact Kickboxing World Champion

2010   Hosted *The Master Method* television program (4 years)

2011   Awarded 5th Degree Black Belt in Hapkido by Grandmaster Jin Pal Kim

2011   Founded The Master Method Academy martial arts academy (4 locations & 1000 students)

2018   Founder & President, Uchudo International Martial Arts Federation

2020   Awarded 10th Degree Black Belt by Grandmaster Keith Nesbitt Sr.

Halls of Fame and Other Honors

2002   Inducted into Karate World Hall of Fame as a Kickboxing Legend

2005   Honored with Official USKBA Trading Card

2008   Inducted into the World Professional Martial Arts Organization Hall of Fame as Master Instructor of the Year, Madison Square Garden, presented by Grandmaster Aaron Banks

2013   Inducted into the International Martial Arts Hall of Fame as Outstanding Martial Arts Leader, Martial Arts World, presented by Grandmaster Y.K. Kim

2019   Honored with the Supreme Grandmaster Black Belt Award, MPower International Association, presented by John Cokinos, CEO

2021   Featured in *The World's Greatest - Vol. 32: Martial Arts Masters Hall of Fame*

2021   Featured in *Changing Lives Series - Vol. 6: Tribute to Ernie Reyes*

Grandmaster Marco has also coached five world champion kickboxers, as well as three international titleholders and three U.S. national champions.

Grandmaster Marco has also coached five world champion kickboxers, as well as three international titleholders and three U.S. national champions.

HELPING OTHERS THROUGH MY EXPERIENCES

In the following years, my belief in myself became even stronger. I went on to train with the Sugar Ray Leonard team in the DC area and eventually won six other world champion titles.

In 2005, I retired from the ring and turned my focus to martial arts instruction, founded The Master Method Academies, Uchudo International Martial Arts Federation and spent my time serving my students and community locally and internationally.

Over the years, I achieved success, not only in the ring but also in other aspects of my life. I now understand that we all benefit through our challenges, and because of this understanding, I'm able to face new challenges more positively and effectively and recognize the benefits of each more quickly.

All of my experiences - the good and the bad - have led me to the life I'm privileged to have today, giving me the necessary tools and belief in my own powers ... not only to create success in my finances, my career, my health, and relationships but most importantly, to enjoy true happiness with my family.

I love my life, and I recognize that I proactively created it. I made a lot of mistakes along the way, but I learned valuable lessons, and every day I find new reasons to be happy and energized about the future. When a new challenge comes my way, I am committed to receiving it humbly, with gratitude and trust, knowing it will undoubtedly lead me down new roads of discovery.

I will always be on my own journey of improving myself, striving to be better today than I was yesterday. However, I can finally say I have left that self-doubting insecure little boy behind and found true peace within myself.

I now invite YOU to explore and apply to your own life - *The Mindset Guide for Winners,* using the method that helped me achieve so much over the years — "The Master Method."

WHY I DEVELOPED THE MASTER METHOD

When I retired from fighting in 2005, I was offered an attractive job with one of the extreme fighting shows on television. Although it was without a doubt a prestigious position with high visibility, I didn't consider it an option. I wanted to make an impact through education. My fighting career was never about titles, money, or fame — it was about striving to achieve, discovering myself, and being the best that I could be in whatever I pursued. I wanted to help others achieve their own successes.

The " Master Method" system goes beyond philosophy and guides you through the powerful steps of applying the wisdom of ancient masters and modern teachers into your daily life.

There are plenty of self-help and motivational books and videos on the market. Many focus on success in business, achieving harmony in relationships, how to improve health, lose weight, or how to find inner peace. My goal with *The Mindset Guide for Winners* is not only to inspire you but also to show you HOW to become successful in *all* areas of your life.

I present the 5-Step Master Method to share years of study and collective wisdom in a single book. This guide will help you create and condition the winning mindset needed to succeed, and it will guide you in maintaining positive thinking when faced with roadblocks and barriers that inevitably present themselves. If I change thousands of lives with this book or merely one life for the better, then I will have reached my highest achievement yet.

HOW TO USE THE MASTER METHOD

The Mindset Guide for Winners contains a step-by-step mindset habit-forming system and important exercises for implementing this proven equation for achieving success. No matter where you are in your life ... young or old ... poor or privileged ... whether you're hoping to make a complete change or simply a few improvements ... following the 5-Step "Master Method" will help give you tools to appreciate and enjoy this one life each of us is given.

As you progress through the chapters you'll learn how the circle of elements in the Master Method are intertwined to work together. You'll also realize the great importance of putting the exercises in the book into practice in your daily life.

Beginning this adventure of new thinking may require frequently referring back to sections of the book to remind you of specific points. But over time, the ideas, concepts, and exercises will become second nature, and before you know it, you'll find the Master Method has become a way of life — a way of life that will empower you to live your dreams with a winning mindset.

WHAT YOU WILL LEARN

The Mindset Guide for Winners comprises a series of 5-steps for achieving your successes over and over again. Following these steps, you will first create a detailed vision of the life of your dreams and your heart's desires. Next, you'll learn and practice techniques to *condition* and strengthen your mind through exercises in gratitude, humility, positivity, faith in your plan, and patience.

Next, you will proactively develop a bulletproof roadmap for your journey with action steps to keep you moving forward toward your dreams. You'll then learn techniques to help you stay on track when you're faced with inevitable challenges, so you can win those battles like a true world champion.

By the final chapter, you'll see how all steps of the Master Method work together, empowering you to take control and create success in every area of your life. We'll also review the complete method and set you up with helpful tools and motivational tips to stay on course and break through barriers.

YOUR JOURNEY BEGINS NOW

Are you ready to open your mind and take control of your future? If so, you're about to embark on an exciting journey ... a journey to a life of peace, success, prosperity, joy, and fulfillment — *your* life. It will be your ideal life; one you create, sculpt, and feel proud of with each small accomplishment. Once you take control, you will have the power to systematically achieve your goals, enhance your health, improve your relationships and finances, and most importantly, strengthen your mind and your spirit.

No matter how many failures you may have suffered ... no matter how bad you feel physically, emotionally, or both ... no matter how many unhappy relationships you've experienced or financial problems you've faced, this can be your new beginning. Even if you feel satisfied with your life already, *The Mindset Guide for Winners* and the Master Method will guide you in making a good life great, or a great life even better!

Let's get started!

STEP 1: DECIDE

DEFINING WHERE YOU ARE & WHERE YOU WANT TO BE

In the late 1980s, one of the greatest kickboxing champions of all time, Bill "Superfoot" Wallace, put on an exhibition in Santiago. For me as a young teen interested in martial arts, it was incredibly exciting to see someone of his caliber. I was completely awestruck and amazed at his talent. I was so inspired by his abilities, I decided at that very moment I wanted to become the world champion. From that day forward, it was all I could think about. I focused on that dream and everything I did in my life became part of staying on my path and working toward that goal.

Of course, when I shared my aspirations with my family, friends and even the martial artists I trained with, most of them told me I was crazy or made fun of me … some even laughed at me! No one even understood why I wanted to do this, much less support me by believing in my dream. Yet, somehow, I didn't allow their reactions to diminish my own conviction. I knew in my heart what I wanted to achieve, and I was going to do whatever it took to accomplish it.

IT'S ALL IN YOUR MIND

We humans can process thousands of thoughts in our brains every single day. Some are passing thoughts that may not hold much significance, such as:

- What to wear
- The weather
- Which shoe to put on first
- Cereal or eggs for breakfast
- Good hair day / bad hair day
- How much coffee to pour into the cup
- Paper or plastic at the grocery store

And other thoughts seem much more significant:

- I hate my job
- I love spending this time with my kids
- How am I going to pay the bills this month
- My spouse is criticizing me again and I hate it
- When I volunteer at the hospital, I feel so happy
- I feel fat and I hate my body
- I don't know what to do with my life

We all process an incalculable variety of thoughts — small, insignificant, quickly passing thoughts, as well as sustained, contemplative and habitual thoughts — and it's impossible to be aware of and monitor every single one of them. But believe it or not, your past thoughts and feelings have influenced the situations and circumstances you're experiencing in the present, and you have the ability and power to shift your thoughts and feelings *now* to create a better future.

"All the breaks you need in life wait within your imagination. Imagination is the workshop of your mind, capable of turning mind and energy into accomplishment and wealth."

— NAPOLEON HILL

The Thought - Feelings - Energy Connection

It begins with a single thought. That thought produces feelings, and those feelings produce energy. Energy — positive or negative — attracts more experiences and circumstances with similar energy. Thus, each person's current reality is the result of thoughts, corresponding feelings, and energy produced in the past.

The thought process, either consciously or unconsciously, leads to the creation of situations, circumstances, relationships, and opportunities in our lives. Many people assume every situation and circumstance they face is random, based on luck or not within their control. So, they live their lives *reactively*, responding to random circumstances, situations, and people, and consequently feeling powerless and at the mercy of fate.

"The universe, from its farthest galaxies to its largest planets, to the tiniest particles in a single atom, exists as energy. Energy never stops. It is constantly changing from one form to another and it is everlasting in time."

— GRANDMASTER MARCO SIES

You Have the Power to Take Control

You have more control over your life than you think! Every thought that flows through our minds produces corresponding feelings, either positive or negative in nature. The feelings we are experiencing will result in energy around us, also positive or negative in nature, which will attract more people, circumstances, and situations with like energy. And so, our feelings and resulting energy are the keys to what ultimately manifests in our lives. And what controls our feelings? Our thoughts, of course.

Cognitive scientists believe at least 95% of all thought is unconscious thought, so in most cases, we are not even aware of our thinking. While most thoughts don't create strong feelings in us one way or another, others can produce strong and powerful feelings that will affect our energy, which in turn affects every situation and circumstance we encounter. So let's talk about energy.

UNDERSTANDING ENERGY

Before we learn anything else about how to achieve a life of success, happiness, and true peace, and before taking the next step in our journey, we must first understand a little about this amazing universe in which we live.

We are energy beings, as is everything around us. If we break down any living or non-living thing into its smallest particles — down to its molecules, atoms, and even the smallest components of those atoms — we are left with the tiniest particles of constantly moving, vibrating energy.

We humans, when broken down into our organs, tissues, and cells, can be broken down into smaller and smaller particles, down to our atoms, and those atoms can be further broken down into their components: protons, neutrons, and electrons.The tiniest of these particles are in a constantly moving vibrational state, thus making every person formed by these particles in a state of vibration as well.

If we look at it very simplistically, like atoms vibrate with the same energy, and they bond to form larger particles. Those like particles complement each other, reproduce, grow, or attract more particles, forming larger and larger particles, and eventually forming non-living things or living beings. This attraction, growth, and energetic structure is the basis for everything that occurs in the universe.

When you, as a human entity, "vibrate" positively or negatively, through your thoughts, feelings, words, or actions, you'll attract more of that similar vibration to your life. This attraction of similar energy and vibration could be in the form of people, situations, or circumstances that will positively or negatively influence your life. Understanding this simple universal concept is the foundation for creating the life you desire.

You Are the Creator of Your Own Reality

YOU have the power to control how you are vibrating, positively or negatively. Therefore, the ability to bring whatever you want to your life is yours. You have the power to create your own wonderful reality, with faith that the universe is on your side.

By using The Master Method as your guide, you'll no longer be a passive spectator or victim of uncontrollable circumstances around you. You'll no longer reactively live a life of randomness and worry. You'll no longer have to hope or wonder if everything is going to turn out okay. Instead, you will develop into an active creator — an inventor of thoughts, feelings, and positive energy that will elevate your state of being. You'll have faith that, whatever experiences you face, you're gaining wisdom and advancing closer and closer to your goals.

It's extremely important to realize your PAST thoughts and feelings have created the situations and circumstances you're experiencing in the present. Your current situation is the result of feelings you've already experienced, and you must remind yourself that those thoughts and feelings *are in the past*. They don't exist right now if you don't let them. More importantly, you have the ability and the power to create a new reality for yourself simply by shifting the way you think. This will change how you feel, and these new positive feelings will result in a positive shift in the people, situations, and circumstances coming into your life. This is worth repeating: *You Are the Creator of Your Reality.*

So, as you read further and begin the exercises in this book, remember the importance energy plays in all you do. In order to construct the life you want in every area (career, finances, relationships, health, and inner peace), you must pay attention to how you are "vibrating." What kind of energy are you emitting? Positive or negative? What are you attracting to your existence?

And so, to summarize: Thoughts alone don't possess much power. However, the *feelings* produced by those thoughts, especially strong feelings, possess the amazing power to change our lives. Those feelings, resulting behaviors, and actions are the key to creating our desired reality. By choosing to "vibrate" positively, we can create positive results and ultimately, a truly amazing life.

The Power of Thought

Everyone talks about the power of positive thinking, but how exactly do we keep our thoughts positive? It would be a nearly impossible mission if we attempted to monitor all thinking. We have constant thoughts running through our brains day and night, and it would be an overwhelming task to try and keep track of them, much less make sure they were all positive. However, paying attention to our *sustained habitual* thought processes is more manageable, and it's actually an important indicator of how we are vibrating and what kind of energy we are attracting.

The easiest way to determine what kind of energy we are transmitting and attracting is simply to ask ourselves: *How am I feeling?*

Answering this most basic question can start to give you a clearer picture of the kind of energy you yourself are creating at this time in your life. Recognizing your feelings and energy is very powerful, and if you find your feelings to be negative, don't worry, because it can all be turned around.

Now that you understand the importance of the thought-feelings-energy connection, let's begin the actual work of changing some of your sustained habitual thought processes for the good!

I DON'T WANT THIS. I DO WANT THAT!

Before navigating toward any destination, you need to know your starting point first. You can then use your compass, map, instructions, or GPS to help get you where you want to go.

Let's begin this journey by acknowledging what your current life situation is and how you feel about each aspect of it. Mark the beginning of your transformation by making a commitment right now to be an active participant in the process.

Write It Down

Your first action in this process of creating the life you desire will be to start a journal. Any blank notebook or paper will work fine to write down your thoughts, reflections, lists, and exercises. The writing process is *essential* as a highly powerful tool in preparing for a life of contentment and achievement. It gives power to your intentions and inspires you to be accountable to yourself.

On the first page of your journal, write a quick brainstorming list of answers to the following Starting Point questions. Read each question, then start writing immediately. Answer with the first thoughts and feelings that come to mind. There are no wrong answers and don't worry about how they're phrased. Your writings are for only *you* to see and evaluate, so it's extremely important to BE HONEST

when answering these questions and others throughout your journaling process. The more honest you are, the more powerful this exercise will be.

EXERCISE: STARTING POINT QUESTIONS

Answer the following questions on page one of your journal. This first page will allow you to evaluate where you are right now in your life. Remember, brainstorm this list fairly quickly, write the thoughts that come to mind first, and be honest. You can write in bullet points, phrases, single words, or full sentences. It's up to you. Just write it down and express it.

- List a few adjectives or phrases to describe the current state of my life.
- How do I feel about my life and current circumstances?
- What do I love about myself? My life?
- What do I NOT love about myself? My life?
- What are my feelings about where I stand in the following areas:

  - Career
  - Finances
  - Relationships
  - Health
  - Inner Peace

Once you've written all you can regarding the different areas of your life, and your feelings about your life, you now have a black and white, hard-copy representation of how you see your life now — your current reality. Believe it or not, this first exercise in your journal will be important in creating the life you dream of, especially if you wrote about areas in your life that you don't like, that give you stress or you wish you could change.

THE LAW OF DUALITY

Recognizing and acknowledging the things in your life you don't like will be significant in your journey because of an important universal law called the Law of Duality or the Law of Opposites. This is the understanding that there is an opposite to everything and that positive and negative give meaning to each other.

If there is an entity of evil, an entity of good exists as well. If you experience

feelings of sadness, be sure you can also experience happiness as well. If you find scarcity in your life, the possibility of abundance also exists. Darkness and light, black and white, high and low, yin and yang … opposites represent the perfect balance and counteraction of all the forces of nature and the universe, and this counteraction of opposite forces and their neutral balance is essential to the creation and sustaining of life.

In our lives, these contrasts allow us to appreciate one or the other end of the spectrum. Knowing that one extreme exists and having experienced that extreme allows us to understand and appreciate the other extreme. In addition, each opposite possesses the ability to change into its counterpart. As easily as we can experience one, it can almost as easily be transformed into the other. Because of this contrast, we can recognize and identify what we want in our lives. By looking at, feeling, and experiencing the things we don't want, we are able to more easily recognize what we do want for ourselves in each of the areas of our lives:

- Career
- Finances
- Relationships
- Health
- Inner Peace

It's amazingly simple to take this first important step in turning your life around. In recognizing what you *don't want*, you'll realize what you *do want*. And once you know what you want, the next step will be learning to positively place your focus on THAT. And then the real fun begins!

EXERCISE: DON'T WANT / DO WANT LIST

We are now going to *organize* the thoughts and feelings you brainstormed about previously, using the Starting Point thoughts in the first exercise of your journal as your guide.

1. Divide your next journal page into 5 sections:

- Career
- Finances
- Relationships
- Health
- Inner Peace

Under each section, using your brainstorm list as a reference, list all of the things in each area that make you unhappy, frustrated or bring you stress — things you would like to eliminate, change or improve. This is your *DON'T WANT* list.

2. On the following page, create your *DO WANT* list. Divide this page into the same five sections, and write a corresponding list of things you do want for each item you listed in your *DON'T WANT* list.

In addition, on your *DO WANT* list, you may add other things you DO want, even if they don't correspond to items on your *DON'T WANT* list. Think about what you are passionate about, what you love, and what you really want for your life in each of the five areas.

DREAM BIG! And don't allow your mind to limit you with thoughts of how you would achieve it, how much it would cost or how much training it would require, etc. Just dream without limits!

Note: *The DON'T WANT list is especially helpful in the transformation process because when we understand what we don't want, we will identify what we DO want by contrast. Then we can learn to place our focus on that, and as a result, gain the ability to turn things around!*

Example:

DON'T WANT	DO WANT
A boss who constantly criticizes me	A boss who praises me
Being overweight and out of shape	Being healthy, fit and at my goal weight
A relationship where I'm feeling empty and sad	A happy, loving and peaceful relationship
Feeling stressed financially	Being financially secure and free
	Owning my dream home
	Start my own business
	Feeling peaceful, happy and content

"Life is a series of experiences, each one of which makes us bigger, even though sometimes it's hard to realize this. For the world was built to develop character, and we must learn that the setbacks and grieves which we endure help us in marching onward."

— HENRY FORD

MOVING FORWARD AND RELEASING

What do you not like about yourself? What don't you like about your life? For some, formulating this list of answers could open up a floodgate of emotions and self-criticism. However, recognizing and acknowledging things you don't like in yourself and in your life is essential in the process of creating the life you want and becoming the person you'd like to become. The awareness of what we don't like allows us to realize what we don't want and, through the laws of duality or opposites, we can then identify what we do want for ourselves. Only then can we begin the process of shifting our focus to moving on.

Please keep in mind that, while recognizing and acknowledging what we don't want is a productive part of the success process, DWELLING on what we don't want so much that we generate and perpetuate an overall sense of negative feelings such as sadness, worry, anger, discouragement, frustration or resentment is not productive. You may experience thoughts such as:

- I hate not having enough money
- I can't afford things I really want
- I don't like the way she treats me
- I can't stand my job
- I hate my body, and nothing works to make it better
- If it weren't for him, I would be so much happier
- I am stuck in a life I can't change

Recognizing and acknowledging these thoughts and feelings are important. The next step, however, is even more important

— MOVE FORWARD AND RELEASE THEM. Use these thoughts and feelings as a springboard to work toward and create what you do want for yourself. You can turn it around if you recognize that you can stop the cycle of perpetuating negativity, and then you'll be on your way to good things.

NEGATIVITY ATTRACTS NEGATIVITY

Allowing our minds to sustain negative thoughts and resulting negative feelings only stimulates the attraction of even more experiences and circumstances with that same energy. Negativity seeks and attracts more negativity. It's that simple.

The more you dwell on what you don't want — think about what you don't want, talk about what you don't want, place blame on others for what you don't want, feel sorry for yourself because of what you don't want — and allow those negative views to bring about more feelings of sadness, anger, and frustration, the more negative feelings and negative energy you will produce. And, ... yes, you know the cycle: the more you will attract circumstances, situations, and people in your life that match that harmful vibration.

You Can Break the Cycle

The great news is the negative cycle CAN be broken! The key to breaking the cycle is in understanding the vital concept I will repeat once again because it's so important:

Your PAST thoughts. feelings and actions have created the situations and circumstances you are experiencing in your present, but you have the ability and power to shift your present thoughts. feelings and actions NOW to create a wonderful future.

You can begin to create a better future for yourself right now. You can begin simply by proactively, intentionally, and *positively* focusing your thoughts in order to feel good. This is another important concept I want you to always remember.

If I had to leave you with only two words on a sticky note to attract the life you desire, I would leave you with these two simple words:

Feel Good.

HOW TO FEEL GOOD

Here's the prescription: Do whatever you can (in a healthy, positive way and within reason, of course!) to consistently create good feelings within yourself.

- Intentionally think good and positive thoughts
- Surround yourself with people you love
- Listen to music you love
- Spend time in nature
- Exercise
- Go to places you enjoy
- Participate in your favorite activities

By maintaining positive energy within yourself, you'll sustain positivity around you. As a result, this positivity will attract even more circumstances, situations, and people matching that good vibration, which will then multiply, giving you even more reasons to feel good. This positive cycle of experiences and feelings will help you move forward on your path to achievement.

There are times, however, when it can be difficult to maintain a positive attitude or sustain positive thoughts and feelings, especially when we experience challenges or unexpected turns in the road. Sometimes, as part of the path we take toward our goals, we experience situations we didn't expect or desire. During these challenging times, it may be necessary to recognize that this set of learning experiences will help us with developing the knowledge, tools, or strength we need to help us further along the way.

You're Only Human

Even the strongest in spirit can become weak and experience feelings of frustration, anger, despair, or defeat. It's perfectly normal to have these feelings. And sometimes, we must allow ourselves these feelings of weakness in order to appreciate our contrasting wonderful feelings of strength. It may even boost our energy and motivation toward striving to maintain our positive feelings once they return. Don't forget, experiencing contrast reminds us of what we do want.

Choose the Positive Path

Do you remember the personal story of my first big American boxing match at the beginning of this book? Some might have let that devastating event end a career. Of course, I suffered feelings of disappointment, disillusionment, anger, and failure as anyone would afterward. But I chose to examine the situation and look for the lessons to be learned. I reminded myself of what I was working towards and I was able to turn it into an experience that would give me tools to get me closer to my destination.

The key is not to allow our low points to become SUSTAINED feelings of negativity. Walk yourself through those natural feelings and consciously make an effort to shift them to a more positive outlook. There are always two choices you can make in every situation you encounter.

Example:

NEGATIVE PATH	VS	POSITIVE PATH
Focus on what you don't like about the situation	VS	Keep a clear picture in your mind of what you really want
Focus on what you don't want to happen	VS	Remind yourself how good it will feel to reach your destination
Dwell on how bad things seem	VS	Look for good in the situation, how it's strengthening you, how you'll benefit later
Feel terrible and blame others for your misery	VS	Focus on feeling good despite the circumstance
Allow fears and worry to distort how you look at the situation	VS	Find an activity and change your focus to something that makes you feel good

Remember, there is *always* a seed of benefit in every situation we encounter, even if you can't see it immediately. Look for it. With patience, time, and shifting your thought habits, it will come to light. So, just like in the old song, accentuate the positive — focus on what you want and choose to FEEL GOOD.

EXERCISE: FEEL GOOD LIST

Next in your journal, start a list of thoughts, things, people and activities that make you feel good, bring you joy, make you smile and give you feelings of happiness. It can be anyone or anything! When you need a boost of positive energy, use this list to remind you, inspire you and motivate you to feel good. Sometimes we need reminders to do the things we enjoy, appreciate the ones we love and allow ourselves time to shift back to a positive frame of mind and heart. Your FEEL GOOD list is personal to you, and *only* you can decide what to include on your list. An example of a Feel Good list is my own, which looks like this:

- Enjoying time and making memories with my family
- Spending time in Hawaii
- Fishing
- Listening to my favorite music
- Experiencing nature - plants, animals, the mountains, the ocean
- Teaching my students
- Meditation and prayer

The only one who can stand in the way of your success, and the only enemy you'll have to defeat on your journey, is *yourself*. Remember, only about 5% of the human mind is conscious thought, and the other 95% is subconscious. These are thoughts and feelings, stored in our brains and based upon experiences from our past, even as far back as infancy. Some believe we are even affected by experiences prior to infancy. Every past experience and all of the thoughts and feelings associated with those experiences are stored in our subconscious minds, and we are not even aware of most of them. By making and referring to your feel-good list often and choosing positive activities, you can begin to create an overall positive and winning mindset just by feeling good.

Break Down Barriers by Feeling Good

If you were to travel back in time and observe your childhood experiences and interactions in detail, it would help you understand why your life is the way it is today, and why you think and respond the way you do in certain situations. Past interactions such as someone telling you you're not good enough or not capable, that in order to have money you must suffer or sacrifice, you can't do this, you can't do that, and so on, all influence how you think and behave now.

" Let the beauty we love, be what we do."

— RUMI

Past negative experiences are the source of many roadblocks and barriers that prevent your success, happiness, and peace. These experiences were imprinted on your subconscious mind, so even if you've consciously forgotten the details of thoughts, feelings, and interactions associated with an event, they're probably with you today and will continue to have an impact unless you're able to identify them, understand them and change them. They'll continue to hold you back from realizing your dreams and achieving a masterpiece life, unless you condition yourself and your mind to turn it around.

Perhaps you never even tried to set goals for yourself because of past negative experiences and the belief that you were not capable, worthy, or deserving. But you can change all of that now, and move forward toward the destination of your ideal life of success, prosperity, happiness, and peace. In subsequent chapters, *The Mindset Guide for Winners* will guide you through The Master Method and the conditioning process to break through those roadblocks and barriers, and this time you WILL follow through.

THE FIVE AREAS OF LIFE

You're well on your way through Step 1 of The Master Method: *Defining Where You Are & Where You Want to Be* . You've learned about positive and negative energy and the Law of Duality. You've identified what you don't want and what you do want. You've examined the power of thought and the thought-feelings-energy connection. We've discussed moving forward and releasing past experiences, as well as choosing the positive path.

In the next chapter, you'll learn to condition your mind for success, but before we go further, let's take a moment to look more specifically at the five main areas of life.

- Career
- Finances
- Relationships
- Health
- Inner Peace

Career

It's interesting that so many people don't even know what it is they love or what it is they would really like to do. They live their lives just going through the motions, reacting to what life throws at them.

Every day they get up, go to work, and are on autopilot most of the time, doing what they're "supposed" to do, but hating each day. They complain about the job and the people they work with, they believe they are overworked and underpaid, and they just plain don't like being there and wish they were doing something else.

Identify Your Passion

If you're really miserable doing what you're doing, stop and allow yourself to think hard about what you would enjoy doing. Search deep within yourself and ask yourself what you truly love. What is your passion? As I mentioned before, dream without limits. What would you love to do, regardless of the requirements, the money or the circumstances? Just ask yourself without limitation, what would truly make you excited and happy to know you could wake up every day and do THAT?

Once you've identified what you would love to do, don't worry about how you're going to get there or how you are going to do it. When you get down about your current job, remember that it doesn't help to allow these bad feelings to continue. You ABSOLUTELY will not change your situation when you're focused on how unhappy you are. In fact, you'll be attracting more of those thoughts and resulting feelings to you, it will affect your actions, your circumstances, and it will virtually ensure you really will be stuck there.

Make the Shift

Now, after the few pages you've read here, you should be aware and realize that being stuck there will be *your choice* if you choose to continue to think negatively and feel bad about the situation. On the other hand, you can choose to shift your energy and begin to look at this job as a stepping stone for your next position, not as a sentence for life. If you choose to do your best with a great attitude in a positive manner, make the most of each moment, and do whatever you can to create positive thoughts, feelings, and vibrational energy within you and around you, everything will change.

From Fast Food to Fast Feet

One of my first jobs as a teenager in Chile was at Mcdonald's. Was this my dream career? Of course not. But rather than focus on how hard the work was each day, I still focused on my goal of becoming a world champion, and I considered this job a stepping stone to a better life. I tried to be the best Mcdonald's employee

ever, knowing this was an important part of creating positive energy within myself and reaching my objective. I read every employee manual. I tried to be the best at every task in the restaurant. I came in early and worked late, and soon I was promoted to manager. I even won Employee of the Year! The point is, whatever you are doing, do it with enthusiasm, a great attitude, and work ethic, and your opportunities will come.

If you visualize what you want, how you really see yourself with the job of your dreams — doing it, loving it, and having the time of your life, whatever your current situation — you'll create positive thoughts and positive feelings will follow.

You'll create feelings of excitement and joy, seeing yourself doing what you love, and you'll vibrate according to the way you feel. This energy will help you feel better about your current situation, but more importantly, it will help you attract everything necessary for you to create the reality you want. If you need to meet people, those people will show up... if you need education or knowledge, you'll see the path for that to happen. If you're a good performer you'll gain the attention of whoever needs to see that, and new opportunities will come your way. By just shifting your thought processes, resulting feelings, and actions, you can begin to attract everything needed to keep moving forward toward your ultimate career.

Finances

Of the five main areas of life, this is probably the area most people put at the top of their list of worries.

- Do I have enough money to pay my bills this month?
- How am I going to pay for this expense?
- Can I afford a new house, new car or college tuition?
- Will I have enough to retire? When can I retire?
- I wish I could just have enough to be debt free.

And on and on. The list of worries about finances can go on forever, and it seems to be a constant concern that never ends for most. My challenge for you now, as you read through the steps of The Master Method, is to change your focus. Change your focus from worry and frustration to focusing on what you really WANT.

But the trick is HOW you do it. You're not truly changing your focus if you go from hating being broke to hoping to not be broke. You must totally shift your focus to the *opposite* of being broke — abundance, wealth, and prosperity!

At first, it may seem impossible, especially if you're trying to figure out how to put

food on the table or cover your bills for this month. However, if you allow yourself to "play the game" with your mind, it will soon become easier to think this way and truly feel excited about it. It will soon become a picture you can easily paint in your mind and it will generate good feelings within you. And remember good feelings are always the goal. You want to generate positive feelings that you can sustain in order to keep your vibrational state positive.

Imagine your finances the way you would like to have them:

- How much money do you have in the bank?
- What does your life look like with the money you desire?
- What are you buying?
- Where are you traveling?
- How do you feel in your prosperity?

By imagining your financial state the way you want it — by playing it like a movie in your mind — you're creating feelings of excitement and happiness. These wonderful feelings will allow you to vibrate in tune with your desires, and you will begin to attract that reality to you. You'll attract the right people, circumstances, and experiences you need to make financial abundance your reality.

Relationships

This area of life is the one that can affect the spectrum of every emotion we can think of in every way possible. Relationships can bring us to the highest of highs and the lowest of lows, more than any other area of our lives. The connection between two people is a wonderful thing, and it begins within each person. If you experience struggles within yourself or you're not at peace with yourself, it makes it very difficult to experience peaceful relationships with others. What happens around you is a vibrational mirror of what is happening inside. If you're having a problem with others, you must first look within yourself and "fix" what is going on in there.

The Blame Game

Many people blame external sources for their misery. Although an external source may be a trigger, YOU are ultimately responsible for allowing it to affect your emotions and choosing which emotion you respond with.

Negative emotions:

- Anger
- Fear
- Resentment
- Jealousy
- Frustration

When you focus on negative emotions, your feelings correspond, you begin to vibrate negatively, and your resulting circumstances will match that. If you continue this negative cycle, you'll continue to attract more thoughts, feelings, people and circumstances to match and support the way you feel.

Similarly, when you focus on the negative qualities of another person you'll often find more things not to like, and it's difficult to get along with anyone if you're focused on what you don't like about them. When you maintain this negative focus, you're not only making it difficult to get along in that relationship, you're also harming yourself overall, by creating negativity that will begin to attract more negative circumstances in other areas of your life as well.

Finding the Good

When you focus on finding the good in another person, that will attract more positive feelings. It will be much easier to get along with someone when you're intent on feeling good and paying attention to the good qualities he or she has. By doing this, you can surround yourself with positive energy, and the other person will see more good in you as well. It's important that YOU are in control of the way you feel, and not allowing external sources to control you.

Positive emotions:

- Love
- Gratitude
- Compassion
- Joy
- Kindness

By looking for the good rather than what you don't like, not only will you be able to understand the other person better, but you'll feel better and handle situations better in the event of a conflict or a disagreement. You'll also inspire the other person to feel better, and you can become the calming breeze for their emotional turmoil.

Never give in to anger, fear, or any other negative emotions. You'll only make the situation worse. It's irrelevant whose fault an issue may be. The presence of any negative emotion, regardless of the trigger, will make it impossible for you to experience positive feelings. Your mind at any given moment can only experience either positive emotions or negative emotions — it can't experience both at the same time. So, by consciously exercising love, kindness, compassion, understanding, gratitude, and joy, even in challenging circumstances, you'll be able to maintain a positive frame of mind and a positive vibration, which will translate into better relationships with everyone around you.

Health

The fourth area of our life is the area we tend to focus on physically. However, in order to truly enjoy good health, we have to understand that health begins in the MIND. As I have stated repeatedly (and I will continue to do so because it's so important!), we are energy beings ... we are constantly vibrating, either positively or negatively, depending on what we are focusing on. And because of this vibration, we are attracting more people, circumstances, and situations that match our energy.

Examples of focusing on sickness:

- Being afraid of getting sick
- Being obsessed with germs
- Constantly talking about our ailments — aches, pains, illness, treatments
- Taking many different kinds of medicine "just in case"

- Always reading or watching TV about illness, sickness, and ailments
- Constantly worrying about whether each ache or pain could mean something terrible

For people who vibrate in this way, it's not surprising when they begin to experience the types of physical ailments they're obsessed about not getting in the first place! At the very least, this way of thinking prevents them from experiencing their maximum potential of good health physically, emotionally, and spiritually.

Practice Good Health

That's right. It takes practice. Of course, it's important when you actually feel ill to seek medical help and listen to your doctor's advice. However, the quality and speed of your healing process will be greatly determined by the way you choose to think and feel during this process. Focus on feeling good; focus on health. Our bodies have an amazing capability to heal, and we have the ability to slow or speed up our own recoveries by the way we choose to focus our thoughts and energy.

It's very difficult for medicine and doctors to help a person whose predominant thoughts are negative in nature. I'm sure you know of someone who always seems to be sick, one illness after another... and if they're not sick, they're worried about becoming sick! They're constantly thinking about illness, all the while creating the perfect opportunity for it to manifest. Now, if you're that person, you CAN stop!

Once again, you are responsible for creating your own reality, so you can start creating a life of good health in your body and mind, simply by focusing your mindset positively.

Examples of healthy thoughts and feelings you can choose to place our focus:

- Visualizing yourself physically strong and healthy
- Picturing yourself attaining your goal weight
- Exercising regularly and enjoying it
- Feeling strong in your body, mind and spirit while experiencing true peace, happiness, laughter and joy
- Telling yourself that you feel great and believing it!

All of these thoughts can also be amplified if you write them down as affirmations, reflect upon them and visualize them. Write them in your journal as statements that are present tense, as if they are occurring at this moment. For example: "I am strong, healthy, and I feel great!" or "I feel so proud of myself for achieving my goal weight!"

You are creating your reality, so do everything you can to feel good right now. Feel the power of the universe manifesting through you. Even if you're experiencing illness or sickness right now, you can change that — not by negating medicine or by refusing help from doctors, but by changing the way you look at things, and changing your thoughts, focus, and behaviors from illness/not feeling well to becoming strong, healthy and feeling great!

Inner Peace

The last area of life is one that every person, without exception, seeks and yearns for. Inner peace is an experience of freedom — freedom from fear and worry, and freedom from the negative influence of destructive thinking. This freedom has its basis in the perfect balance between you and the universe. It comes from the understanding that you are not singular or alone; you're so important and you're part of the whole. You contribute vitally to its existence and to everything and everyone around you.

Understanding Energy Centers

Human energy is believed to be stored and distributed through energy centers within the body. It's important that your main energy centers — Emotional, Intellectual, Physical, and Sexual — are in harmony in order for energy to be used efficiently. If you shift too much energy to one of these centers, the other centers won't operate as they should. For example, if you're highly stressed, you may get physically tired, even if you haven't done anything physically. It's a case of your Emotional center draining energy from your Physical center. Have you noticed that someone may get a bit grumpy or short-tempered after they've been working hard academically such as studying for an upcoming test or completing a big research project? That's because the Intellectual center has been zapping strength from the Emotional center.

Another aspect to achieving inner peace is having faith and really trusting that everything will go according to our intentions in the long run. We must know that all that's required is to maintain a positive mindset and feel good, no matter what challenges arise or what the current circumstances are. Intentionally and proactively enjoy the journey and remember that mindset is creating your future!

TAKING THE FIRST STEP

Suppose you got on an airplane, asked the pilot where it was going, and he answered, "Hmmmm, I don't know." Would you continue on to your seat and take that flight? Probably not. Similarly, would you make a trip by getting into your car and just start driving, without deciding first where you want to go? You may drive for a while, make random turns and end up in the middle of nowhere. Needless to say, this would not be the most efficient way to take a trip, and it certainly is no way to live your life!

Where Are You Headed?

The first step in creating your ideal life is to DECIDE what you want. What is your ideal life? Where do you want to go? When you don't have a destination and a clear picture in your mind, you'll either continue on in your current undesirable circumstances, or you'll wander aimlessly, ending up in random places and situations haphazardly. Or even worse, you could also end up being part of someone else's plan and living your life by default. If you know where you want to go, you can now take steps to prepare and move toward your destination.

Unclutter Your Mind

Sometimes it's hard to decide exactly where you want to go because your mind is filled with clutter from the past, present, and future — regrets, worries, what you have to get done on your to-do list, or what you haven't done yet. From there, doubts can creep in: Am I even worthy of where I want to go, or worthy of improving my life? Should I follow the path of my parents, my teachers, or someone important in my life, even if I realize a relationship may have been unhealthy for me? Sometimes we seek to gain the approval of others and follow a path we think is expected of them, although it's not necessarily a path that feels right. Or you may have fear that prevents you from attempting to improve your life — fear of failure, rejection, roadblocks, or having to move out of your comfort zone and challenging yourself.

What's very important to realize is that ALL THE MIND-CLUTTER CAN BE OVERCOME if you recognize it's there — identify it, acknowledge it, and consciously and systematically put it aside. In the following chapter, **Step 2: Conditioning Your Mind for the WIN**, you'll learn how to overcome clutter and roadblocks, and free your mind. The clutter can be cleaned out so it will no longer hinder your success. You'll be empowered to do whatever it takes to get to your destination, and there will be nothing to stop you anymore!

Find Your Passion

You may have several things you want to accomplish. But regardless, your first step is the same — you must first find your passion deep within you by asking yourself what you really, really want. Sometimes you'll know the answer without hesitation. Other times you may have to go through a process of soul-searching and introspective evaluation to decide exactly what you want. Nevertheless, you must come to the point where you absolutely know without a doubt, with determination and conviction, what you seek to accomplish. And once you've answered this question, the next step will be the key to your success.

Visualization is Key

Now that you've answered the question, "What do I really want?" you must picture it in your mind. Every single day. Several times a day, close your eyes and form a clear image of what your accomplishment will look like. Form a literal mental picture. Have faith and really believe in the images your mind is projecting, so the corresponding positive feelings will result. You may even pretend it's your current reality. You must really feel this new reality and allow yourself to sense the happiness, joy, satisfaction, and excitement of attaining your success for this exercise to be effective.

By visualizing success, you'll be creating a vibrational match in accordance with your desires. In doing this, you will begin to attract people, experiences, and even knowledge that align with your focus. You'll find that opportunities will arise, when you seek the answers they will be shown, and the path becomes clearer to achieve success, happiness, and balance in all areas of your life.

I was first exposed to the power of visualization and meditation when I was young, perhaps 14 years old, while attending a philosophy school in Santiago, Chile. One day, our instructor asked us to get into a comfortable position and, through very slow breathing, quiet our minds and relax our bodies. He guided us to visualize a quiet and peaceful setting. Prior to this, we heard cars driving and honking, and all of the city noise of busy Santiago. However at the moment we all joined in collective visualization, the city became silent. It lasted for about thirty seconds, and I realized we have so much power within us. We are the architects of our lives, and we are capable of creating and shaping our existence. It was then that I truly understood we have to be able to visualize our success first before we can experience it.

Practice Makes Perfect

In order to create positive feelings of excitement and anticipation, take a little time every day to visualize what you want to become, what you want to do, and what you want to acquire — the house you want, the career you want, the relationship you wish for, the money you desire.

Take a moment to relax your entire mind and body, and focus your thoughts on your goal. Feel it in your hands. Smell it. Listen to the sounds. Taste it. Experience it with all of your senses, and make it a reality in your mind at that moment. At the end of this chapter, there's an exercise for this crucial part of the process of The Master Method. I'll guide you through a simple and easy meditation. I'll also describe a couple of exercises you must follow conscientiously, as they are significant steps in mastering success.

Visual Stimulators

That said, it's not enough just to think about success. You must truly feel it with your whole being so that your feelings and energetic vibration are in alignment with your vision of how you want your life to be.

When I decided I wanted to be a kickboxing world champion, I worked extremely hard to physically develop myself into that champion. I knew it would take time, discipline, and extra-human effort, but that wasn't enough. I consciously and consistently took the time to visualize it. I could see my achievement vividly, I could feel the hot lights, I could smell the sweat, and I could hear the crowd cheering. On the walls in my room were posters of champions I admired to remind me of where I was headed. I surrounded myself with the greatness I desired. Every morning, every afternoon, and every night I saw the pictures of those champions, and in doing so, I was unknowingly reinforcing my visualization exercises. Every time I looked at those images, I felt optimistic. It renewed my energies and I was recharged with joy and happiness.

Whether your goals are huge, life-altering aspirations, or smaller daily things to accomplish, the universal laws, principles, essential elements, and steps you need to follow to achieve them are the same. These principles are quite simple, and over time will result in inevitable success as long as they're understood and followed faithfully.

IT'S TIME TO DECIDE

Are you ready to decide with certainty where you want to go? And once you decide, are you committed to actually doing it? It's not enough to just make the decision that you want something. And reading this book won't help if you don't take action.

The Mindset Guide for Winners was written to guide you through The Master Method process to proactively achieve your own personal successes, not just by giving you concepts to read and experiences to relate to, but by guiding you through your own journey of intention and implementation so you WILL reach your destination.

In the next chapter, we talk about conditioning the mind. With each chapter you read, allow some time for introspection and to really think about what you've read and how it relates to you and your own personal situation. Start meditating and visualizing your goals. Write in your journal, and read what you've written as often as possible. Immerse yourself in this intentional process. All of these action steps truly hold power.

If you wish, journal and write more than just the exercises suggested here. Put down on paper your thoughts throughout the process — your dreams and your plans. Draw pictures, cut and paste photos — anything that comes to mind. As I said before, the act of writing things down and reading what you have written is exceptionally powerful. It's a vital action step in creating intention and accountability, and keeping your thoughts and feelings positive so you can continue moving forward, making progress, and creating your successes.

Once you're able to DECIDE and VISUALIZE that clear picture in your mind of what you truly want, your thoughts, feelings, actions, and energy will be positive and focused on achieving the life you desire. You'll be amazed at the power of taking this very first step on your path. You'll feel a sense of excitement, anticipation, and pride that you have taken action and officially begun your journey to achieve your goals.

EXERCISE: DETAILING YOUR "DO WANT" LIST

Some individuals have a very clear picture of what they want to accomplish, so it's easy for them to create and describe images in their minds. For other people, it's a little more difficult to determine what they want, articulate their desires, or form images of those desires. They might know they want a better life, but they don't know exactly what to do to make it better. Many times they just don't like their present state of affairs and they think that's just "how it is" or they don't feel worthy to live a better life. Sometimes they don't feel entitled to be at peace with themselves or in harmony with the world around them. This book—and even this very first exercise—can completely change those perceptions of feeling lost, confused, or undeserving.

In your journal, do your best to describe IN DETAIL how you would like things to be in each of the five areas of your life — career, finances, relationships, health, and inner peace. Using your "Do Want" list from the previous exercise as your guide, begin to add more and more detail to your descriptions so you have the most vivid picture possible of your future.

At this point, you might even dedicate a separate page for each area, to allow for as much detailed description as possible. This is where you can have some fun! Go ahead and describe your dream life in detail: colors, sounds, smells, sensations, interactions, what you're wearing, how you look, etc., because these written details will help you create visual details in your mind when you meditate and carry out your visualization exercises. The more detail you can include, the easier it will be to generate those positive images and feelings that will create the energy you need to attract all those good things to your life.

EXERCISE: VISUALIZATION MEDITATION

Using your detailed "Do Want" list and descriptions you wrote for each of your five life areas, the following exercise will now take you to that place and allow you to experience your goals in your mind through visualization. This exercise should be repeated as often as possible so you can constantly create positive feelings of anticipation, happiness, and excitement within yourself.

Find a place that makes you feel physically comfortable and relaxed. It may be someplace quiet, a favorite chair, your bed, the backyard, or even a nice hot bath. Choose a place where you can take a few minutes to reflect — a place where you can be in connection with the inner you, with no distractions from the outside world. Even if you're not able to get to your favorite place, you can do this anywhere — your desk at work, parked in your car (never while driving, please), or in a waiting room. Wherever it may be, the important thing is you're taking a moment to focus your mind and your thoughts by following these steps:

- Sit or lie down and enjoy the peacefulness of being alone with your thoughts.
- Take a moment and close your eyes and allow your eyelids to relax.
- Regardless of your present circumstances or what you were doing a moment ago, take all of those thoughts out of your mind. Forget your list of things to do or worries you may have, and release all logical thoughts and feelings about your current life. Empty yourself of all preconceived and limiting ideas of what you can or can't do. Imagine yourself empty and open.
- Very slowly, breathe in through your nose, filling your lungs, and then slowly exhale through your mouth. Repeat these slow, soft intentional breaths.
- With each breath, feel each part of your body let go and relax, from the top of your head, all the way down to the tips of your toes, and allow your mind to quiet, letting go of any outside thoughts.
- Now, fill the openness of your mind with the images, sounds, smells, and sensations of the life you want to live.
- One by one, imagine each of the areas of your life exactly the way you wrote about them in your detailed description. Paint a vivid picture in your mind of your career... your finances ... your relationships ... your health ... your inner peace...

- For each area of your life: Where are you? What are you doing? What are you wearing? Who are you interacting with? What sounds do you hear? Allow yourself to see every detail and experience how it feels to be exactly where you want to be.

- Feel the satisfaction, excitement, and joy of being in the profession you love. Allow yourself to feel the happiness of wealth and abundance. Feel the love of the significant person in your life and how wonderful it is to be in tune with each other. Feel the accomplishment of reaching your health and fitness goals and feeling better than you ever have in your life. Feel the absolute peace and contentment from deep within yourself and the joy of knowing you can endure anything because of this peace.

- Remember, it's crucial to be VERY specific with the details in your visualizations. These details help to create a clear picture in your mind and, as a result, allow positive feelings to emerge — the feelings of reaching your goal. These feelings will in turn create the energy that will affect your behaviors, thinking processes, and actions you take that will clear your path and open the doors to the experiences, people, and opportunities necessary to actually make it a reality.

The most important aspect of your visualization process is creating with your thoughts, the feelings that are going to inspire you, drive you, and put you in a winning mindset. This mindset will inspire positive action and attract positive experiences to your life.

Your goal is to feel good. If negative thoughts take over your mind, refer to your Feel Good list, your visualizations, and your writings, and stay focused on what you want, rather than what you don't like about your present situation. Keep visualizing the outcome you desire and how it feels to get there.

"*Ask, and it shall be given to you; seek, and ye shall find; knock, and it shall be opened unto you ... for every one that asketh receiveth; and he that seeketh findeth; and to him that knocketh, it shall be opened.*"

— JESUS

Surround Yourself

What also helps in the visualization process is posting pictures, symbols, and reminders of what you want to accomplish. A photo representing your dream job, a place you would love to visit, the house you dream of, or the financial status you would like to achieve. Write a check to yourself for the amount of a paycheck you'd like to receive. Post these things in a place where you can see them every day, and when things don't feel good or you're experiencing other types of negative emotions, refer to your writings and visual reminders. All of these small things can help to steer you back to a positive state of mind so you can continue moving positively toward the things you want.

Let's Move On

I hope you've made the decision to move forward with actions, and by now, you should be feeling eagerness and excitement about your future prospects. Now that you've looked at your present situation, thought about what you don't want and what you do want, you've written it all down and created a picture in your mind of your ideal life, it's time to fully condition your mind to keep you on the path to success. Let's begin chapter two!

"In order to think positively, you must condition your mind through life- long practice."

— GRANDMASTER MARCO SIES

STEP 2: CONDITION

CONDITIONING YOUR MIND FOR THE WIN

NOW THAT YOU'VE DECIDED WHAT YOU WANT

Good! You've finished the first chapter of *The Mindset Guide for Winners* and Step 1 of The Master Method, and you've made a strong start on your path to proactively achieving your goals. So far you have:

- Taken an insightful look at your current situation
- Made a list of what you don't want and what you do want in the five areas of your life
- Learned how thoughts invoke feelings, which produce negative or positive energy, and you know this means you are the creator of your own reality
- Explored some of the ways to create positive energy within you and around you

- Discovered the value and power of visualization in forming a precise picture of your desired destination in your mind

CONDITIONING YOUR MIND FOR SUCCESS

In this chapter, you'll be introduced to the concept of *conditioning* your mind, just as an athlete conditions his or her body for a race, a match, a fight or other sporting event. I do realize it's sometimes easier said than done when someone tells you to just feel good or think good thoughts or stay positive. Often our intent and desire are there and we really want to feel good, but life happens, and we find ourselves back in a negative frame of mind and feeling not so good. No one wishes to think negatively or feel bad, and no one intentionally tries to do so. But all too often it has become a habitual way of thinking and being, and this is the cycle that must be broken. Awareness and intentions will be your superpower to overcome this.

That's All Well and Good, But ...

It's easy to feel good and think positively when things are going well. But in order to feel good and maintain a positive frame of mind in the midst of challenges and circumstances we may not like or anticipate, it requires a conscious, intentional, and consistent conditioning of the mind. In much the same way we condition our bodies through exercise and a healthful diet in order to build strength and endurance, or simply to remain healthy, there are also ways of conditioning our minds for strength, endurance, health, and most importantly, inner peace. It doesn't just happen. We MAKE it happen. Conditioning our minds and achieving true serenity within us is in itself a success. However, creating success in every area of your life can become limitless once you've achieved inner tranquility by practicing CONSISTENTLY to condition your mind.

You Can Change Your Thinking

In order to maintain strength, endurance, and health in our mindset, we must make this conditioning a life-long practice. Just like anything else in life, there is no magic light switch or overnight success potion to achieve success. The consistent and daily conditioning of your mind is key, and it must become a way of life — not something you practice for one day or week and expect to get results. But if you're willing to learn and take action consistently, I promise you'll find these techniques do become second nature and the positive attitude you create will pay off in every aspect of your life.

Once you understand and incorporate the essential elements of conditioning your mind, you will always possess the tools to overcome your roadblocks, barriers, and fears. Some of your barriers may be obvious challenges or situations you need to overcome. Other barriers may root deep in your subconscious mind, originating from neural pathways —nerve tracts that connect one part of the nervous system with another and are critically important in learning — formed in early childhood or perhaps even before that, and you're not even aware they are there. But with constant, consistent conditioning and nurturing, your psyche can emerge strong, healthy, and ready to face any challenge.

THE ESSENTIAL ELEMENTS FOR A POSITIVE MINDSET

As part of The Master Method to achieving success, I have compiled a list of essential elements that are not only vital for the attainment of success, but these components will allow you to create a life of inner peace, joy, and happiness. Understanding, practicing, and making these elements part of who you are will allow you to create the ideal life you deserve.

As you read further, you'll learn the importance of each of these elements, as well as share valuable exercises and practical ways to not only understand the elements but also allow them to become second nature. By consistently practicing the conditioning exercises, remaining conscious of the essential elements, and consistently reminding yourself to maintain or shift your mindset in a positive direction, a success mindset will become a part of your being. You'll naturally think and feel positive, and success will become your new way of living.

The following is the list of essential elements for conditioning our minds to maintain a healthy and positive mindset. When we achieve this higher state and sustain thoughts and feelings consistent with each of these elements, we allow ourselves to feel and surround ourselves with positive energy. As a result, our paths begin to illuminate, the right relationships and opportunities cross our paths, and the creating process for achievement flows more easily.

Now, you may be expecting these elements to be along the lines of self-confidence, persistence, discipline, vision, willpower, resolve, assertiveness, and other characteristics usually associated with the subject of success. Those are all important attributes needed to achieve. However, before those characteristics, there are a few foundational elements that need to exist first.

The Master Method Essential Elements for Conditioning the Mind

- Gratitude
- Humility
- Positivity
- Faith
- Patience

In the following pages, each of these elements will be discussed in detail, along with exercises that will help develop and enrich each of these qualities within you.

ESSENTIAL ELEMENT # 1: GRATITUDE

I've been teaching martial arts for more than 35 years now, and I'm often asked, "How do you do it?" People want to know how I'm able to make each class an exciting class with enthusiasm and high energy, all day, every day. Even when I have a challenging group, with students that may be a little more difficult to teach, I see a great opportunity to become a better martial arts master. I feel grateful and remind myself of this gratitude every day. Maintaining energy and enthusiasm despite the challenges makes me a better instructor. Not giving in to what may be a frustrating situation or struggling student and creatively rising above the difficulties to stay enthusiastic and positive gives me a sense of accomplishment and satisfaction in every class. And for that, I'm extremely grateful.

Reminding myself before each class that I am grateful for being a martial arts instructor, keeps me in a positive frame of mind to lead the best session possible. I remind myself that this could be a student's first-class or their last class, and it will all depend on how I teach it. I try to maintain a level of enthusiasm as if this class were the last opportunity I may ever have to teach. The students deserve my best. I'm grateful for the challenges because they increase my knowledge, strength, and ability to strive for improvement in becoming a better master, instructor, and person.

A Powerful Emotion

Gratitude is a surprisingly powerful emotion that elevates your state of mind. As I've said before, and will repeat again, this higher state of mind will provide you with incredible strength and the positive mindset to influence all the events in your life. Even if you encounter problems, finding the seed of benefit and feeling grateful despite those challenges will keep positivity swirling around you and this energy will in turn help you find, recognize, and create more beneficial experiences coming your way.

Sure, there will be difficult times when the unhealthy part of your mind will tug at you, and you may find yourself seeing the negative side of things, feeling frustrated, thinking about how much you dislike something or dwelling on how difficult a task is and all the reasons you can't and won't succeed. You're certainly not alone in these kinds of thoughts and feelings, or in finding yourself behaving in a way you wish you could change.

We All Face Barriers

As I mentioned previously, for a wide variety of reasons, we have a certain amount of clutter personal to us in our minds. And we all have circumstances from the past that challenge our way of thinking and pull us down a path of negative thoughts and feelings. You may have had parents who criticized or discouraged you. You may have had hurtful childhood experiences — physical or emotional — that made you feel fearful or undeserving. Perhaps you grew up in a financial struggle or in an environment immersed in negativity. All of your experiences early in life programmed you to think, behave and react to experiences in a particular way. You may have even had a very positive childhood but, for whatever reason, you continue to struggle with following through on a plan for success. Maybe you have trouble taking action and sustaining your momentum toward your goal.

A lifetime of experiences contributes to possibly delaying or blocking your successes. Individuals manifest their mind clutter in different ways (fear, anxiety, indifference, procrastination, not taking action because the task seems too difficult), but it all basically boils down to this:

Sustained negative thoughts and feelings will prevent us from progressing down the path to our goals.

We all have some type of mind clutter from personal development that can pull us into a temporary or sustained negative frame of mind. This clutter must be cleaned up in order to achieve the life you desire. But there is good news! These barriers can be overcome. In fact, just the ability to catch yourself falling into any negative thinking, being aware of this, and recognizing the negative impact of sustaining this type of thought is a huge step in overcoming and conquering this unhealthy habit.

The duality of knowing what you don't want contrasted with what you're striving to become often increases the motivation to get there, as well as the desire to feel the appreciation and excitement of the accomplishment once you do get there. It gives you the springboard to create intentions and take action based on those intentions. Practicing gratitude is a particularly effective device in overcoming the barriers of negative thinking and mind clutter.

Practice Makes Progress

For some, gratitude is not a quality that comes naturally or easily, and for these individuals, the mindset of gratitude must be practiced. The more you repeat thoughts of gratitude, the more you'll actually experience feelings of gratitude, and the more positive your mindset will become, creating and attracting more positive experiences, which will start the constructive cycle all over again. By proactively looking for and finding things to be grateful for and *practicing* thoughts of gratitude, eventually gratitude will become an emotion from your heart automatically, and it will become a part of who you are deep inside. The more you practice thoughts of appreciation and gratitude, the more you'll find to be grateful for.

My Daily Gratitudes

Every day when I wake up, I practice my visualizations. This is a process I have used since I was a teenager, where I intently focus on how I want my life to be. I visualize even to the smallest detail, the images, smells, sounds, and feelings of how I desire the parts of my life to be. When I'm projecting these images and desires, I feel grateful knowing it is coming, and in my visualization, I feel the gratitude as if I already have it, even though the realization of that desire has not yet come to be. I create the thoughts and feelings in my mind, and I feel the emotions in my body as if it were already a reality. I smell it ... I listen to it ... I feel it in my hands ... I hear the sounds ... and I feel grateful for that moment and for the experience. I feel the excitement of being there, even if it is only in my mind for now. Then, after I come out of my goal visualization, I feel excited that it's coming, and then I place my focus on what I am already grateful for — my current life and all of the blessings I am receiving.

Recognize and Acknowledge

A central part of the process of conditioning your mind is proactively recognizing and acknowledging the things you're grateful for in your current situation. It can be your kids — their smiles, laughter, or funny things they do ... a relationship — how much you love that person and how he or she enriches your life … having a roof over your head — this in itself is something to be grateful for, when you realize how many don't even have that … having food to eat — remember how fortunate we are in the small things we take for granted … your job — just having a job in recent times is something to appreciate given how many have suffered as a result of the weak economy… your health — many take this for granted as well, but we should all be thankful for each and every day we spend on this earth. Remember, no matter how bad things get, and as difficult as things may be for you, there is always someone who is less fortunate and going through something worse. There is always something for you to be grateful for.

In this process, when you consistently focus on what you're grateful for, you will create positivity within your mind, which will then contribute to cascades of feelings, energy, and experiences that will result if you make this a habit. Use what you already have to create a positive frame of mind and remember, when you feel good, you vibrate in alignment with the life you want. You'll start creating the energy necessary to pave the path of people, opportunities, experiences, and circumstances to get you there.

EXERCISE: THE DAILY GRATITUDES

When you wake up in the mornings, make a habit of proactively thinking about what you're grateful for before you begin your day. Actively look for it and acknowledge it in your mind. Write down if you want its power to be amplified even more.

Do this before or after your visualization exercises, and any time throughout your day.

Make your gratitude exercise a practice you do as often as possible. Our minds are churning constantly, so why not fill them with thoughts that will actually benefit you? Strive for gratitude to become your natural way of thinking and feeling, even if it feels difficult and unnatural, or you don't believe you have much to be grateful for. At first, you may need to make a conscious effort in remembering this exercise or to search your life for what you even feel grateful for. You may even need to write a daily to-do list and add *"remember all I am grateful for"* as part of that list. If this is difficult, search for things at that moment such as appreciation for a sunny day, or a person who had a smile on their face that you thought was nice. If you search hard enough, there will be something to appreciate.

In time, the conscious exercise of listing these gratitudes will evolve into your entire outlook. You'll naturally seek the good in any person or situation and feel gratitude for his or her existence. You'll eventually possess the ability to instinctively recognize and feel thankful for even the most challenging people and situations, because you know they're strengthening you and gaining helpful tools to reach the goals and life you desire.

Each day, write a new daily gratitudes list in your journal. At the top of your list, start with what you're most grateful for today — family, friends, your work, your health, all of the things you enjoy, and the things that are going well. Be grateful for everyday things ... for a beautiful sunrise or sunset ... for being able to see, hear and experience this wonderful world. It might be as simple as a friendly waitress at your favorite coffee shop, or time for a short walk on your day off. Be grateful for your mere existence and for being able to experience all life has to offer. Be grateful now, with the faith that you'll receive what you are seeking. Feel the excitement of anticipating and knowing it is coming.

"The voice of wisdom cannot be heard, except to the ears of a mind that is open and humble."

— GRANDMASTER MARCO SIES

When Things Aren't Perfect

Sometimes, however, you may have to be creative when looking for daily gratitudes. For example, you may not be in your dream career position right now. In fact, you may not even enjoy your work right now. But if you allow yourself to be thankful that this job is ultimately helping you gain experience or is serving as a stepping-stone or means of support to get to your ultimate career, then those positive thoughts will allow positive feelings to flow. Write those things down on your list.

We all have bad days and difficult periods, and on these occasions, it's especially important to find seeds of goodness, digging deep to find a way to feel grateful for something. Remind yourself that in these challenges, you will grow, develop strength, gain knowledge, and receive tools to help you in your journey toward your goals. As you learned earlier, every experience — good and bad — has a benefit. Remind yourself of this every time you face adversity, and feel thankful for the strength and wisdom you are gaining because of it.

ESSENTIAL ELEMENT # 2: HUMILITY

Humility - "freedom from pride or arrogance; modesty; the quality or state of being humble; not thinking that you are better than others; being open to receiving knowledge or wisdom."

Imagine for a moment you wanted to climb Mount Everest. Right now, you're wearing shorts and a T-shirt. You haven't researched, trained, or prepared in any way, and you have abso-lutely no climbing equipment or cold-weather clothing. It would be extremely difficult for you to survive a journey like this if you go into it unprepared. You must learn to climb, train, get the necessary clothes and tools, and perhaps gather a team of individuals to help get you there. You may have to learn from others or face challenges while you acquire the necessary knowledge and physical training, but you keep your ultimate goal in mind and do whatever it takes to reach the summit. In this scenario, you humbly accept the challenges as necessary experiences that are giving you the tools to become stronger and more equipped to face the climb ahead.

"True wisdom comes to each of us when we realize how little we understand about life, ourselves, and the world around us."

— SOCRATES

Likewise, when you're heading for a destination of success in your life, every situation you encounter will either teach you something you need to know or give you the insight or understanding you need along your journey to success. Humbly accepting every experience as having a seed of benefit will help you remain in a positive frame of mind, despite facing disappointments or defeat. Even if this process takes a few steps within your mind, finding a way to accept the experience humbly will help you overcome the adversity more quickly. Avoid feeling resentful, defensive or angry about challenges and roadblocks. Create and maintain the mindset to move forward constructively, rather than placing blame or dwelling on the negative.

The Silver Lining is Real

There is always a benefit or opportunity in every circumstance you face. Look for it! The benefit can come in many different forms. It may be strengthening your spirit, developing your character or it could be teaching you how to effectively deal with hardship or misfortune. These are all instruments that will help you in later steps on your journey. Maintain a sense of humility through rough patches so you can maximize your benefits from them. Humility will always contribute to your positive mindset and result in the positive energy around you.

Losing is Nothing More Than a Big Part of Winning

In some situations, you may feel as though you've "lost." Don't let a negative event or setback stop your momentum. Humbly accept it as part of the process, and remind yourself that you're becoming stronger, wiser, and more equipped to continue on.

Whenever you face disappointment, just remind yourself that losing is just a part of learning to win. You will win in the end, as long as you don't give up.

How to Practice Humility

How can you practice being humble? Here are a few practical suggestions for ways to weave the virtue of humility into your nature.

- Empty your mind - imagine it being an empty cup ready to fill.
- Receive knowledge and help from others openly and with a fresh mind. You may learn something valuable that will help you later. Even if it's something you've heard before or think you already know, receive it openly with gratitude, as a reinforcement of your knowledge.
- Take these kinds of thoughts out of your mind:
- How difficult it is
- Why it may not work
- Reasons you shouldn't move forward
- I don't have the money
- I don't have the experience
- I don't have the expertise
- Open yourself to every experience, good or bad - take it as the wisdom of learning what *to* do or what *not* to do. Remember, every experience has value.
- Open yourself to receive the benefit of every experience - actively look for the benefit and identify it.

- Allow yourself to think thoughts and feel feelings of gratitude for the experience.

The first item on the list is particularly important. Before you even begin your journey, imagine you are emptying yourself of any preconceived ideas, negative experiences, or anything cluttering your mind that may hinder the receipt of valuable knowledge. Take out of your mind all the reasons why something may not work or how difficult it's going to be. The universe will give you all the answers you need to accomplish your goal. It's your job to find them.

Open yourself up to receive new knowledge presented to you, for these contain character-strengthening experiences and wisdom that will help you in the attainment of your goal. Allow yourself to receive and benefit from any information, so you don't waste a single opportunity or experience. Avoid at all costs the attitude that you already know everything you need to know or that you don't have room for another way of looking at things.

Be a Receiver

Imagine a glass of juice filled to the middle, and you try to pour another full glass of water into it. The glass will overflow, and much of it will go to waste. There's not enough room for both the juice and the water. Humility is much like that — being humble (emptying yourself) allows you to make room for insights, perceptions, and understanding. Being able to empty yourself, so when you fill your glass, you can keep every bit of valuable knowledge and not waste a single drop. Sometimes you may not immediately grasp the teachings of a situation, but don't waste the opportunity when it is shown to you.

Be humble. It will put you in an open, positive frame of mind that will allow you to advance toward your dreams with as few stumbling blocks as possible. Once you become receptive to the seeds of benefit in all circumstances, your path will become clearer with each life experience.

EXERCISE: LIST OF BENEFITS

In your journal, create a list of recent challenges you've faced. Now empty yourself of any negative thoughts or preconceived ideas about how this challenge affected you or will affect you. For each challenge, list as many benefits as you can that resulted or could result from this experience. What tools did you or could you acquire from this challenge?

Think very carefully about the positive effects of each challenge and how each situation could be beneficial. Come from a place of objective humility when you think about your answers.

Examples of benefits could be:

- Strengthening of your spirit
- Appreciation of something or someone who makes you feel good (the opposite of the challenging situation)
- Teaching patience
- The circumstance led you down a path toward a person who could benefit you in some way

- You learned something from that experience that will help you handle challenges in the future
- The wisdom you gained from that adversity will allow you to help someone else someday

ESSENTIAL ELEMENT # 3: POSITIVITY

The third essential element in The Master Method for conditioning your mind for success is positivity. Positive thinking is the fuel needed for your desires to become reality. If we use the road trip analogy again, at this point in your trip, you've chosen your destination so you know where you're going. You're now preparing yourself so you won't get lost on your journey, and you want to get there in the most efficient manner possible. You have the vehicle to get you there, but you must have the right fuel to keep the vehicle running smoothly and efficiently, so you won't break down along the way.

The same is true to experience success in any area of your life — you must nourish yourself physically, emotionally, and spiritually so you can avoid breaking down. While it seems somewhat easy to identify ways to remain healthy physically, it can be much more complicated to identify how to obtain and maintain emotional and spiritual health.

From the Heart

"Positive thinking" is a phrase that's been used and reused so much we often forget what it truly means and how powerful it really is. Thinking positively is not just a superficial catchphrase we can lightly gloss over or a concept we can try for a minute, and then wonder why we get frustrated when it doesn't seem to be working. Positivity must become a way of life, despite difficult circumstances. It can't be demonstrated just in words and actions, but in feelings existing deep within our hearts. With true positive thinking, you can create positive feelings, which create positive energy ... and that energy attracts and manifests positive results.

Remember what we learned about the thoughts-feelings-energy connection? Energy is always vibrating, and we choose to vibrate either positively or negatively, according to the way we sustain our thoughts and resulting feelings. Reflective of the way we are vibrating (either positively or negatively), we will continue to perpetuate into our lives, good experiences or bad experiences ... good results or bad results ... success or failure. The reality we create for ourselves begins with a single thought, which creates feelings, and those feelings influence our behaviors, interactions, decisions, experiences and circumstances we live with. The thoughts-feelings-energy connection influences everything around us.

You Can't Fool Yourself

Sometimes people think that by doing something nice, despite their true feelings of negativity beneath the gesture, they'll achieve positive results. The act of doing something nice for someone is great, but if deep inside you feel negative feelings, such as anger, jealousy or resentment, then you're not being sincere, especially with yourself. These feelings will only create more negativity unless you can find a way to honestly feel good about your deed. Doing something thoughtful for another person is always a good thing, but it *really* makes a difference when you sincerely feel good when you do it.

Your True Feelings

Imagine yourself in a situation where you have to face something difficult, like a major setback in a big project, or something unexpected that wasn't part of your plan. For most people, the first natural internal reaction is to feel bad or experience fear or doubt. You then attempt to think positively and mask what you're really feeling by pretending to feel good. You tell yourself and others around you that you're okay. You tell them you're thinking positively, although deep inside, you don't actually feel that way. Although what you're saying on the surface is positive, your true feelings are those of fear, doubt, frustration, and insecurity.

These true and deep feelings are what you're actually projecting, and since these real feelings are negative in origin, ultimately, they will not benefit you. All too often a person temporarily thinks positively but is unable to sustain those thoughts and feelings the minute he or she experiences disappointment. Subsequently, discouragement spirals downward into feelings of worry, frustration, unworthiness, and perhaps hopelessness or even anger.

How to Reset Your Default for Positivity

You want true positive thinking and feeling good to become second nature, so you no longer have to consciously choose between thinking positively or negatively, or feeling good or feeling bad. Your goal is for positivity and feeling good to become your default way of thinking and feeling, so your energetic vibration will align with the experiences, people, and opportunities that will help you be where you want to be in every area of your life.

So how can you accomplish this? Understanding the concept is a good start, but now you must master the process of *how* to achieve this quality within yourself. Most importantly, mastering the art of positive thinking and feeling good during difficult times is the challenge. It's easy to feel good and think positively when everything is wonderful. This is natural and effortless. However, when we reach a roadblock or perceived failure, it can send us into a tailspin from which it may be hard to recover.

Emotional Roots

Understanding the roots of your thoughts and emotions will be an important key to overcoming these difficult times that challenge your positive state. Achieving and maintaining a positive frame of mind when you're faced with difficult situations may feel impossible, especially when you're in the midst of a challenge.

Before you can eliminate negative thoughts and emotions, you must first be able to identify them and understand them. Why are you experiencing them in the first place? Why do you feel this way and someone else doesn't? What is the root cause? The answer is within you.

The cause of your negative emotion is NOT the situation itself, a person, or a particular circumstance happening outside of you. The roots of your emotions are deep within you, but ultimately, you are responsible for how you choose to let them manifest. You *allow* yourself to feel negative emotions as a reaction to things happening outside of you, and then you react according to those emotions. You always have the power to choose different, more positive emotions, even if this is a process you have to consciously remind yourself of and walk yourself through. It's not a light switch, it is a process.

If you're feeling a negative emotion (frustrated, angry, worried, hopeless, etc.) stop and analyze the feeling. Try to identify what that feeling is, and what within you is making you feel that way. This self-awareness is the first step in taking control.

Are you afraid of failing? Remember, failure is a big part of success, and it's more often than not, an unavoidable part of the process. So if you understand that and don't allow it to be your final destination, it will only be one of the challenges you experience and overcome along the way to achieving your goals.

Don't let temporary defeat get to you. Remember it's temporary, and it lets you know you need to tune up your plans. It teaches you something or allows you to experience something necessary in order to become successful.

As I mentioned before, feel gratitude for the knowledge and experiences presented to you, even if it appears as a temporary defeat. Without it, your success would be impossible. When you experience a temporary defeat, keep the end result in your mind, no matter how distant it may seem. The timing of nature and the universe is not our timing, and success may be just around the corner.

Do you fall into a habit of negative feelings because of repeated negative experiences as a child? Unfortunately, many of us experience negativity as a child — whether intended or not — in the form of discouragement from our parents, teachers, siblings or other children. Perhaps you were told you weren't smart, or you weren't attractive or you'd never make anything of yourself. Or maybe you were compared to a brother or sister, or simply ignored, making you feel unloved.

These feelings of unworthiness can have a long-lasting effect on anyone, even if these experiences came at a very young age. The resulting feelings and self-esteem issues root deep within our subconscious minds and they can affect how we behave years and even decades later, without us even realizing it.

Diffuse Negative Tendencies

Don't repress or ignore the roots of your emotions. Allow yourself to recognize what you're feeling and really try to understand where it comes from. Only then can you diffuse its power. If you don't go through this process, these negative emotions will inevitably come back again — and even stronger. Ignoring our emotions is like blowing air into a balloon. Over time, emotions accumulate. They build up more and more and, eventually, just as a balloon would pop when it can't accumulate any more air, you'll reach your breaking point in an explosion of emotion.

Making the effort to consciously and consistently monitor the way you think and feel is fundamental in the process of understanding your thoughts and emotions. Once you're able to identify your thoughts and feelings and understand where they come from, you'll have the ability to eliminate the power they have over you and you'll choose to "walk through" and eliminate those negative feelings. You will then choose to think and truly feel positive instead.

You can now allow the healthy part of your mind to take over. With the ability to understand yourself, shifting negative thoughts and feelings will eventually become automatic, and positive thinking and feeling good will become second nature.

The Master's Way

The ultimate accomplishment is when you know no other way but positivity, inside and out. This is when you've truly mastered yourself. You've not only mastered your mind, but you've also mastered your true highest self, your essence. This is the place of true masters and a place every being should strive for. Regardless of how long it may take, mastering yourself —your highest self — should always be the goal.

The mere attempt and process of sincerely trying to master ourselves truly makes us better. The first step in the process is to master your mind — shifting your thought process and the way you feel. As we've discussed, when you master your thoughts and you feel good, your interactions with others will be positive. You possess enthusiasm that becomes contagious. Everyone prefers to be around a person with eagerness and enthusiasm. They'll want to be around you because your positive energy makes them feel good. People will want to do business with you. Your colleagues will develop trust in you and a loyalty to you. In their subconscious minds, they want to be part of your happiness and your victories, so they too can feel happy and victorious.

So, *choose* to think positively, feel good, and act accordingly. *Choose* to smile, show enthusiasm, and strive to always do your best. These qualities are valuable fuel that will propel you more quickly along the path to your goals.

Don't Let Stumbling Blocks Trip You Up

Remember, in the process of accomplishing anything, you may find yourself face-to-face with disappointment or difficulties. When this happens, you must not forget that all things you encounter are preparing you for the accomplishment you're seeking. Keep the end result in sight — your goal, your accomplishment. Don't allow setbacks to activate the unhealthy side of your mind and sustain thoughts and feelings of frustration, worry, or fear.

When disappointment or unpleasant things come your way, as soon as you feel negative emotions overtaking you, acknowledge them as unhealthy thoughts and feelings, recognize where they came from, and make a proactive decision to shift them. Shift your negative feelings to positive ones by consciously moving from thinking about what you *don't* want to what you *do* want. From what you don't like about that situation to reminding yourself of what you're working toward and how this situation will strengthen you.

Find the positive seed that's there for you to benefit from. Sometimes you'll see it immediately. Other times, you may not understand it for a while. But no matter how long it takes for it to appear, the seed of benefit is always there. It may be giving you the tools necessary to succeed in the next step of your journey to success, or it may be giving you the knowledge that's needed to understand and master the unhealthy part of your thought process. Some situations may simply serve the purpose of showing you what you *don't* want, so you can identify and work toward what you *do* want more efficiently and effectively from that point forward.

"Every situation has the seed of something positive that will come out of it — a benefit of equal or greater value to the challenge you faced."

— NAPOLEON HILL

Whatever You Look for, You Will Find

If you look at any situation, you may find good, positive and pleasant things, and you may find bad, negative and unpleasant things as well. Likewise, you'll find the same dichotomy with people you encounter in your life. You may see wonderful qualities and characteristics you love about them, and you may see their flaws and qualities you don't like. It all depends on what you focus on and the kind of eyes you're using to see them — negative eyes or positive eyes. What are you looking for and what do you choose to see?

It has been said that if you sustain a particular way of thinking for a period of at least seventeen seconds, it will attract more and more thoughts with the same vibrational match. A sustained positive thought will create a chain reaction of more positive thoughts, resulting in positive energy, behaviors, actions, and experiences, thus creating more and more positive energy and experiences. In the same way, sustained negative thoughts and feelings create negative energy and negative experiences.

If you enter a situation or an interaction with an eye for the negative, you will absolutely find everything negative and unpleasant about the situation or the person. Negative feelings will form within you, and this will in turn attract more negativity, creating a negative cycle. It's a simple universal law.

Expect Good Things

However, if you choose to look through positive eyes, look for something positive and stay focused on that — regardless of the situation or the person you're dealing with — you'll be amazed at the outcome. Your choice to see the good in any person or situation will result in positive feelings within you, which will produce positive feelings and actions in the other person as well. Your choice to see the good will result in more good coming to you. By choosing to see the good, you'll be able to think good things and, most importantly, feel good. And feeling good will create a positive cycle of events that will allow your dreams to become reality.

Dealing with Difficult People

Sometimes you may face extreme difficulty in recognizing what could possibly be good about a difficult circumstance or person you're dealing with. The unhealthy part of your mind allows you to wonder why in the world you've been placed in this terrible situation, or why this horribly difficult person is someone you have to deal with.

These are the times when you have to really dig deep and truly test your strength. Access all of your power and remind yourself to shift your thoughts and energy to a positive state, so you can react with positivity.

Make the conscious choice to not let this person or situation influence your thoughts and emotions in a negative way. YOU control your own mind and how you will react. Don't let a negative individual or interaction take control, or allow a situation to spiral into an escalated situation. Stay focused on positive actions and reactions such as calmness, patience, and even caring and compassion. If the situation did escalate negatively, step away from the interaction, allowing yourself time to cool down and letting your mind return to a neutral state — a state where you're not angry, frustrated, or stressed anymore. In order to do this, take a few minutes with no distractions, so your mind can really settle, and it won't have the opportunity to return to that negative state.

Hit Replay and Reset

When you find yourself more comfortable, replay the interaction in your mind and consciously put into practice the concept of self-discipline. Don't let your mind go back to the negative state of anger or frustration.

Empty yourself of judgment, and with all of the compassion in your heart, focus only on how you could have handled the situation differently in a more positive way. You can only control your own actions, so only think about what YOU could have done differently to make the situation better.

Imagine it vividly in your mind. Play it like a movie in which you are the director and the main character. Use this edited replay version as your intention for any future interactions that may occur. By seeing yourself handling a situation positively in your mind, you now have the tools to proactively steer difficult interactions in a positive way.

Take the Compassionate Road

Practice love, understanding, and compassion. It's much easier to keep yourself vibrating in a positive way when you do. In fact, love is the highest, strongest, and most powerful of all emotions and energetic vibrations. Be sure you don't get distracted in this exercise and fall into negative judgment and allow yourself to return to an unhealthy frame of mind. It's imperative you practice self-discipline and stay focused on positivity.

We are all faced daily with people and circumstances that can challenge our peace and positive mental attitude. When dealing with a difficult individual, try to look beyond superficial words and actions and understand the underlying motives for his or her behavior — the real reason behind the words and actions. Perhaps he is ill ... or just received bad news — or maybe she has an unkind boss or a difficult situation at home to deal with. When you have compassion, it's easier to think of how you could have handled the situation in a more positive way, or how you proactively plan to in the future.

Project Composure

Practice will help you gain self-discipline in shifting your frame of mind from negativity to feelings of love, understanding, and compassion. In this state, you're able to realize that the harmful words you are hearing come from someone who doesn't know how much he is also hurting himself. Through your compassion, understand the person's pain and try to rise above the negativity by not giving in to anger and frustration. Don't let your ego control you. Even if you have to use strong words to deal with a situation, make sure you're calm inside, and project composure to the person in front of you. Try to become a calming breeze to him or her. Let the person know you're not there to hurt them but to help them succeed. This is an important step that can return both of you to a positive state of mind.

By taking this approach, you'll feel much better about the situation and heal yourself much faster in the process. This will result in shifting your thoughts and feelings into a positive state now and may even help you shift to positivity sooner the next time you encounter a problem. Your mind will be stronger, and you'll be even better equipped to handle difficult circumstances in the future.

As you know by now, in every situation we come across, there is some seed of benefit — something to gain. You're gaining knowledge about yourself, someone else, or about what your next step on your path should be. You may be gaining tools or strengthening your character or your spirit. And so you see, there is a reason to experience every situation because it's part of your passage to success.

"Anger and intolerance are the enemies of correct understanding."

— GANDHI

EXERCISE: PLAY MOVIES IN YOUR MIND

Previously, you were introduced to the concept of visualization. Be sure to practice it, no matter how things are going around you. Every day, set aside some time to just close your eyes and relax. Find a quiet place if you can. If not, practice it wherever you are.

When you wake up in the morning, before you retire at night, and anytime you can find time throughout the day, close your eyes and focus again on what you want. Play it like a movie in your mind, and allow yourself to experience even the smallest details of how you want your life to be. Don't let your current circumstances or problems take your mind away from what you really want.

Have fun and enjoy your visualization. Don't forget, the key is to paint the picture in your mind in such detail, you feel the emotions of already having achieved. It's so important you allow yourself to feel good. Experience all of the elements of how you want your life to be so you can elicit good feelings within you. These feelings will allow you to begin vibrating in tune with your desires and as a result, you'll be in the frame of mind to make them a reality–your ideas will flow, you'll take consistent action, your inspiration and motivation will find solutions, and you'll find yourself crossing paths with the right people and opportunities.

This exercise does not have to take long, but it is powerful. And for it to be effective, you must be consistent in your practice and make these exercises a habit.

After you finish, don't worry about if and when the things you visualize will materialize. Simply TRUST that you're now paving the path, you're taking the positive steps, conditioning your mind, moving forward, and everything you need to create the life you desire will be shown to you.

ESSENTIAL ELEMENT # 4: FAITH

In conditioning your mind for success and creating a "mindset for winners"– we've said there are five essential elements you must weave into your fiber of being. The absence of even one of them will result in either failure to accomplish your goals, delaying them, or failure to maintain them for any period of time. And so we come to the fourth essential element in conditioning your mind for success — FAITH...the belief, trust, and knowing that you will achieve.

Once you've determined what it is you want and you have established that intention, without this fourth essential element of faith, you lack the fuel to truly propel you forward. It's somewhat like declaring you want something but negating that desire because you're not sure you deserve it or can achieve it.

If you know what you want with absolute certainty, you must completely believe you can accomplish it with every molecule of your being. You must have FAITH that your success is coming. This step may be the most difficult for some, but it's something that can be overcome through awareness and consistent internal work. It's like strengthening and conditioning a muscle that's never been used.

Believe It, Achieve It

The concept is simple. If you truly believe it, you will achieve it. You'll find a way. And similarly, if you believe something is impossible or too hard to accomplish, and you have doubts, it will be extremely difficult or impossible to achieve. You'll give up along the way, or you won't even begin.

If you firmly believe you're on your way to accomplishing your goal, you will take the necessary steps to get there, you'll do whatever it takes, and you won't give up when you experience challenges.

After accomplishing your first step of deciding with certainty what it is you really want, ultimately, your faith will determine if you'll realize your goal or not. This is the most critical essential element needed to become successful in the accomplishment of *any* of your goals.

"Faith" in this case, does not simply refer to a religious faith, although if your religious faith is true and pure, that will certainly help and can be combined with the essential element of faith we speak of here. The element of faith in conditioning your mind for success is the strong, unwavering, and steady belief that, no matter what circumstances you're faced with, you'll reach your goal or achieve anything in your life you desire.

Know It in Your Heart

It is not enough, however, to just believe you can do it. You must really KNOW without a doubt that you WILL do it no matter what it takes! Faith is a deep-down belief that you will reach your goal, even when you experience challenges. Faith is also the acceptance of every experience — good and bad — as a necessary part of the process. It's effortless to have faith when things are going just as you planned. However, when you experience an unexpected turn or delay, if you face a frustrating situation, or if you make a failed attempt at a task, this is when faith can be challenged. And this is *exactly* when faith is most important.

Receive everything that comes your way with faith and the strong unwavering belief that every experience is leading you to your goal. Every experience is preparing you and teaches you. Every experience is providing you with the wisdom, strength, and tools needed to reach that wonderful place—the place of realization of your desires and the accomplishment of your dreams.

Finding Your Faith

In order to find and maintain your faith in achieving success, empty yourself of all preconceived ideas of how hard an undertaking might be. Remove thoughts of how you're not good enough or don't have enough money, how difficult it might be … or any negative musings that could block your success. It's particularly easy to find excuses as to why something won't work, why you're not progressing, or why you're not trying in the first place. All of these roadblocks and detours can challenge your faith, and they will keep you from moving forward.

However, once you recognize your barriers and realize you may be falling into a negative pattern of thinking, the process can be proactively shifted in a positive direction.

Here are some methods to help you find your faith:

- Empty yourself of negative thoughts.
- Be aware of negative thoughts coming to you.
- Recognize them.
- Identify them.
- Let them go! Actually visualize yourself throwing them into a black hole never to return.
- Replace these thoughts with positive reminders to yourself that success is coming no matter what.
- Remind yourself that this "detour" is part of the process, and it's giving you the tools and the strength needed to progress toward your goal. (It is NOT a reason to give up or feel defeated.)
- Remind yourself in writing. In your journal, keep a list of your intentions (ONLY the POSITIVE reminders of what is coming to you!)
- Read this list of intentions often (especially when you've experienced a temporary setback or negative experience.)
- Read your list out loud. The spoken word adds more fuel to the flame of your desires. It is so powerful.
- Feel the feelings of excitement that each intention will bring you. Read it and feel the positive emotions as if you've already received each of them.

"Your living is determined not so much by what life brings you as by the attitude you bring to life; not so much by what happens to you as by the way your mind looks at what happens."

— KAHLIL GIBRAN

Faith allows you to feel happy despite circumstances that may not initially appear to be positive. Faith is believing what you want is already yours. It might take a minute, or it might take years to accomplish. Either way, faith is knowing it IS going to happen, and it will happen in the right time.

Have Faith in The Universe

Remember, nature, and the universe are perfect. Choose to have faith in yourself. Have faith in the universe, nature, a higher power, supreme intelligence, or whatever you believe in. No matter what you may face along the path to your destination, unwavering faith makes you untouchable. Have faith that every experience will benefit you in some way, and what you gain from each one is necessary to get you to your destination. When you're vibrating in a certain way, whether you're feeling good or feeling bad, the universe is going to correspond to that vibration and send you more people, situations, and circumstances to match that vibration. Choose good vibrations.

Remember when I mentioned that I had even been homeless for a time? That's a perfect example of how things will come to you if you stay positive and have faith. Even though I was sleeping on the street and at times having to ask complete strangers for a quarter or anything they could spare so I could buy food, I never lost my faith in the universe. Soon, I did find a job doing night cleaning at a gym. But the meager paycheck was not enough to cover rent for an apartment. One of the gym staff heard I was looking for a cheap place to stay, and he opened his home to me, gave me a room, and said I could pay him later. I will always be grateful for this gesture. Now I had a job, a place to sleep and soon more good things came my way. My boss at the gym, seeing how hard I worked and hearing about my circumstances, generously offered to give me an old car he had, saying I could pay him back when my situation improved. So now I had a job, a place to sleep, and the transportation to get to a second job, where I could earn more and I eventually had enough to rent an apartment. My positivity brought good things, and that continued the cycle of more and more good feelings and good things happening as a result.

Don't forget, it's your decision to vibrate positively or negatively. Choose to do it positively, and positive results will follow.

"Our greatest weakness lies in giving up. The most certain way to succeed is always to try just one more time."

— THOMAS EDISON

Understanding True Faith

Sometimes people think they have faith when in reality, they don't. In their thoughts, prayers, or meditations they focus on a particular burden (or many burdens) and they ask to please be relieved of the burden because of how much pain, stress, or frustration it's causing them. They focus on their burdens and the negative feelings, asking for them to go away.

For example, someone may be struggling with money and financial concerns and says a prayer to please NOT let them experience this lack of money and suffering anymore. They have so many bills and not enough money in the bank to pay them. They don't want to be in debt anymore. They're focused on the pain and suffering of debt and ask for the suffering to be taken away. With this kind of presentation, experiencing positive results is difficult. First, this person is so focused on what they don't want, there's no room for thoughts of what they DO want and how wonderful that would feel. Second, by placing focus on the suffering and what they want to go away, they remain in a negative state of vibrational energy. Thoughts are still on misfortune and the negative feelings it has caused, and so it's difficult to leave that cycle of thoughts, feelings, and experiences that come as a result. Proactively and consistently changing the focus of thoughts and prayers to the goal of what is deeply desired will shift the energy and results in another direction—a positive direction.

Opposites of Faith

Another example of someone's misconception of faith is someone who faithfully prays or meditates and asks for something as a goal. They visualize it wonderfully, picture it, feel it, and imagine being in that achievement for a fleeting moment of excitement. As they finish picturing it, the following thought process begins: "How in the world am I going to attain that?" which leads to a list of reasons why it's going to be so difficult, or perhaps even impossible. The downward thought process includes ideas like

- I don't have enough money.
- I don't know how to accomplish this.
- What if I'm not smart enough?
- I'm not good-looking.
- I don't deserve that.
- I don't have enough time to work on it.
- What are other people going to think?
- That is going to be so difficult!
- I never get what I want, so why try?

These are the examples of the "opposites of faith." Thinking like this will automatically create a path of resistance to your desires, and this path will lead to negative circumstances, situations, and experiences, which will delay your process or even take you in the opposite direction, making your success impossible.

Everything you want and desire is within your grasp. The process is quite simple: First, you have to want. Then you have to believe. Then you can receive and achieve. If you look at something as being impossible, for you, it really will be impossible. By focusing on obstacles, you can't truly picture success in your mind, and you create a swirl of negative energy and doubt. You vibrate on that frequency, and you continue to focus on every obstacle or every excuse as to why you can't do it. It's the negative cycle of failure.

Ask and You Will Receive

In many ancient teachings, and particularly in the teachings of Jesus, he said when you ask, it's already yours, and the Father already knows what you want before you even ask. You just have to have faith that you'll receive it, and you WILL receive it.

When you have these thoughts and feelings, the universe and your actions will align with making it happen. Everything you need will materialize through your thoughts, ideas, consistent action, and positive situations and opportunities that result. You will create the way to make your journey to success possible.

Have faith that all of the people, situations, and experiences you need to be successful will be presented to you at the right time on your path to your desires. Stay focused on what you asked for. Take consistent action. Have faith and feel good — feel happy it is coming.

Keeping Your Faith

Of course, planning your course of action is necessary, and there are steps and sub-steps you must follow to accomplish your goals. But you must follow those steps with faith and without fear. Maintaining a strong belief throughout your journey will keep you moving forward, despite any unexpected events and challenges. Nature and the universe in all its wisdom, will provide everything you need, at the right time.

If you wish to grow a peach tree, there are a number of steps you must follow, as well as the tools and supplies that are required. Once you plan, prepare, and follow the correct steps to plant and nourish the seed, it will grow. Nature takes care of that in the proper time. If you check on it immediately the following day, and you don't see the tree, you wouldn't just walk away discouraged because your tree didn't simply appear with peaches all over it! This is when you need to have your unwavering faith. This is when you know there cannot be any other way. The tree needs time to grow, but it's going to grow. Your peach tree will be there bearing its fruit … in its destined time.

When you experience challenges or feelings of doubt, impatience, or discouragement, that's when you must use the power of your positive thinking to intentionally and consciously shift your thoughts. As we learned earlier, shifting your thoughts will shift your feelings ... which will shift your energy... and ultimately shift your experiences. Your success is already on its way. You just have to be ready to receive it and have the FAITH to believe it's already yours.

ESSENTIAL ELEMENT #5: PATIENCE

My path to becoming a kickboxing world champion was not one I traveled overnight. I learned from ancient masters, contemporary success teachers, coaches, trainers, and my own mistakes and triumphs. But I'm able to share all these things with you today because of what I learned on my path to achieving my dream of becoming not only a kickboxing world champion, but a seven-time world champion!

The fifth and final essential foundational element for conditioning the mind is patience. Patience was a quality I learned all too well through my own journey. As I've looked back and contemplated the importance of all five of the essential elements, I realized patience was one of the most difficult but vital for me.

Patience goes hand in hand with faith. The element of patience will allow you to endure whatever time it will take and whatever work is required to get where you're going. As I trained physically, mentally, and spiritually to become a world champion, there was always a burning desire within me that kept me focused, disciplined, and committed. The road was a long one, but I knew I wouldn't stop until I achieved the title. Looking back on each step I took along the way, I see the purpose of each minute, hour, day, month, and year it took me to accomplish my dreams. I learned to look for and recognize the tools and strength I gained from each experience, hardship, and setback as well as each small triumph. Sometimes, the benefits aren't understood until later, especially the events that initially felt like detours or failures. But looking back on all of it, I understand, and now I use those experiences and wisdom to help others on their journeys.

Finding Joy in the Process

The art of patience can be difficult to master, especially when we feel so excited about the life we are working toward. Not rushing the perfect timing of the universe, and knowing success will come exactly when it's supposed to, is in itself a challenge. Of course, you always continue to work toward your goal and do what you need to do in order to maintain forward momentum, but at the same time, you must have patience and must develop the ability to be still when action is not required. In addition, if you're working toward mastering the foundation of all five essential elements, you'll come to find joy in the *process* of creating your ideal life. You'll find reasons to be happy and thankful in the moment, NOT just waiting to experience your true happiness only when your goal is reached. Make the most of and find joy in each present moment. Work on what you need to, but also make sure you do things daily to feel good.

As we've discussed (and it's repeated often because it's so important!), when you already know what you want with certainty, your job is to create a positive vibrational state within yourself, in tune with your positive desires, so you can create the most efficient path to making them a reality.

When your energy aligns with your desires, the essential element of patience enables you to maintain your faith and allow the universe time to present you with everything you need exactly when you need it. It may work on a timeline slightly different from yours, so the key is never to doubt your success is coming, and patiently move forward with what you need to be doing!

Placing Your Order

Imagine you are shopping online for things you love. You've been browsing, admiring each and every item, and you've bookmarked the pages of the items you just can't do without. Let's say it's Friday afternoon, around 4:00 pm. You've decided that today is the day and now is the time to place your order! You grab your credit card and happily complete your order at approximately 4:05 pm. and you're excited that your items will be delivered to your house sometime soon. You know it's coming, and you're excited!

Now, let's say at 4:15 pm — just ten minutes later — you're wondering where your stuff is and why it's taking so long. You impatiently look at your watch, pace around your house, look out the window, and you get worried the items may not even be coming. You call the store to complain because you haven't received your products yet and you ask the representative if she's absolutely sure they really will be sent. This sounds pretty silly, right? However, it illustrates the point of how we often decide what we want, we're excited about it at first, then for a variety of reasons we get impatient and we start to doubt and wonder if what we have asked for will even materialize.

In our example, when your order was placed, it would require some time for it to be processed, filled, and delivered. Time is needed to log the order, access the product, pack it, wrap it, and mail it or put it on a truck for delivery. Always remember, once you "place your order," your job is to just feel happy and excited that your order is on its way! You don't have to doubt it or wonder about it. It's ordered and paid for! Have patience knowing it will get to you just as soon as possible — in the time it takes for the particular order to be processed. Some orders can be filled more quickly than others. But once you place the order, just relax and know it will arrive.

Be Joyful While You Wait

I mentioned before that sometimes we need to sit back and be still when action is not required. However, how do we know when action is NOT required? This may be difficult to determine, especially when we want so badly to achieve something and we are working extremely hard to make it happen. In working so hard, sometimes we turn it into a tedious, painful process. There was a time when people believed that unless the process was difficult and painful, the reward was undeserved. You know — no pain, no gain.

"There is nothing that wastes the body like worry, and who has any faith in God should be ashamed to worry about anything whatsoever." —

— GANDHI

"Working" toward something wonderful and joyful should feel wonderful and joyful. The most efficient path toward your goal shouldn't be painful and tedious. Yes, there will be times when hard work and self-discipline are required, but the focus on the joy of what you're working toward should allow you to keep a positive frame of mind throughout the journey. Otherwise, it may not be the right path or the most efficient path for you.

When you're vibrating in tune with your desires and the universe, sometimes NO work is required, and we need to simply sit back, observe and watch for the path to be shown to us. We don't have to worry and think about which path to take. We just know the next step on our path toward our destination will be illuminated when it is the right time. This "illumination" may take the form of meeting at exactly the right moment with the right person who will help advance you toward your goal. It may be a circumstance presented to you that just feels so right, and there is absolutely no question in your mind it's the right choice. As long as you're vibrating positively, your process shouldn't involve tedious work that makes you feel miserable. The correct path will FEEL right.

Big Orders Don't Take Longer

It doesn't matter how big or small your goals are. Those measurements of magnitude live only in our minds, when actually in terms of delivery by the universe, it doesn't matter. We often think if a goal is bigger, it must be more difficult to acquire. However, in order for ANYTHING to materialize in our lives, big or small, it will be born in the same way — as a result of our thoughts and corresponding vibrational state. Our job is to formulate a clear picture of what we want, and then do whatever we need to do to maintain a positive mindset and energy. And when we face detours, delays, or roadblocks, we must remind ourselves we are gaining tools and strength. Seek and find the seeds of benefit, then relax and have patience.

The Limitations of Logic

As humans, our minds are always active. We are always looking for solutions to problems, and searching for logical answers to questions. In our rush to achieve success as quickly as possible, we forget about patience and forget we shouldn't be forcing things to happen before it's time. Sometimes we seek answers that lead us in the right direction, but other times the harder we try to seek logical answers, the more difficult it becomes to find them, and we end up losing our good judgment. We are cerebrally looking for answers, and trying to almost scientifically decide where we need to proceed next on our path. In those moments, we may be motivated by frustration, desperation, impatience, or other negative emotions, and we can't make decisions wisely. Most people use logic and conscious reasoning to find answers when there are times when it may be better to find the answers in another way. Logic has many limitations — it's limited to the information provided by the senses, and sometimes the knowledge we need is found beyond the senses.

"I hear and I forget ... I see and I Remember ... I do and I understand."

— ANCIENT CHINESE PROVERB

As part of the process of developing the essential element of patience in The Master Method, we must gain a little understanding of *knowledge*, and the three ways in which we acquire knowledge.

The Acquisition of Knowledge

There are three types of knowledge we acquire in a variety of ways:

- Knowledge through senses
- Knowledge through experience
- Knowledge through intuition

The first type is the knowledge we gain through our senses. This is the knowledge we are able to process from what we see, hear, touch, and taste. All of this knowledge gives us information we process in our brains, in order to understand the matter in front of us.

The second kind of knowledge is the knowledge we gain through experience. By *experiencing*, we learn and gain knowledge we will not forget because it is stored in our memories of experiences and in our subconscious minds. Although we may not consciously remember an experience, our subconscious mind never forgets.

The third type of knowledge is gained through intuition. This is the knowledge gained through our "extra" sense and it guides us through our lives. Intuition takes us beyond what we can see and beyond our logical thought. We can't confirm or see the answer; we just know. Intuition is the feeling inside ... the feeling you get without logic or judgment. Sometimes all logical evidence points you in one direction, but your intuition takes you in another.

Trust Your Intuition

When you let your *mind* work with your intuition, it's not your intuition working anymore, but your brain ... your logic.

Intuition is the most powerful of all knowledge. It's not based on the senses, but on the true essence of the matter, which is not always understandable by the brain or logical thought. Intuition has no limitations with time, and it's connected to a higher plane of existence. Your intuition is in direct connection with the universe, nature, supreme power, or supreme intelligence. When you truly learn to use your intuition, an incredible universal source of knowledge is available to you for guidance.

If you're faced with a decision at a crossroads, let your intuition tell you which way is the right way. One way will always instinctively feel better than the other. As long as you're truly using your intuition and not your logical thought, you'll know which path to take. It may even turn out to be a path you least expected, but if you truly trust your intuition in making your decision, it will prove to be the path that was meant to lead you to your destination.

If you were to test the accuracy of your true intuition, you would be amazed to realize, without the logic of the mind clouding a decision, the right answer is always simple. As long as you put aside any logical thoughts and preconceived ideas of what you THINK is the right thing to do, you can learn to discover and feel the incredible power of your intuition.

If you reach a point where you're not sure of the next step to take, don't try to rush the answer. Rushing to move forward and desperately seeking the answer will not make it suddenly appear. It may even lead to impulsive decisions that may delay your process. Sometimes you need to just wait … patiently. Sit back, clear and relax your mind, and watch, almost like watching a movie… and see how the next step naturally unfolds in front of you. When the time is right, and when you're ready to receive it, the next step will be shown to you. Always keep your end result in mind, be happy you're on your way to receiving it, and have faith and patience that the best path will be presented to you exactly when it should.

EXERCISE: DON'T SWEAT THE SMALL STUFF

The exercise of patience can be extremely difficult. The mind is always in a hurry, wanting things done right away or wanting answers immediately, even if we're not ready to receive them. We always want to force nature to give us what we want when we want it, and we often forget nature's timing is not always our timing.

One way to exercise patience is to practice with little things. For example, waiting in line at the grocery store, or stopping at a red light are perfect opportunities to practice the art of patience. Allowing yourself to feel irritated or desperate in these situations never helps things move faster. In fact, by giving in to negative emotions, you're setting yourself up to attract more circumstances that will frustrate you and delay you. Then you find yourself in a negative state that continues to create negative emotions within you. Make a conscious decision to shift that energy.

Practice keeping your thoughts and emotions positive throughout your day, large and small — especially in situations when you need to wait or when you're delayed, or in a hurry to get somewhere. When you feel negative emotions surfacing, recognize them, and take a moment to intentionally slow down and pause. Take a few deep breaths ... relax your mind, remind yourself that this is out of your control, and it's okay. This situation is not worth stealing your peace. Place your thoughts on something that makes you feel good such as something you're looking forward to, or someone who gives you joy, and focus your attention on shifting your thoughts and emotions positively. Let go of your tension. Choose to feel good in those moments, and let those moments pass.

It's time to add a new list to your journal — a list of little exercises and strategies you plan on using to develop your patience. Write this patience exercise list and refer to it regularly to remind yourself of things you plan to do, especially during those moments when you're feeling impatient.

Remember — strive to make every present moment of your life positive using your foundational essential elements of gratitude, humility, positivity, faith, and patience. Even if you experience difficulties, you have the power to shift back to a positive mindset, overcoming your challenges more quickly, and staying on course to reach your destination.

"There is no logical way to the discovery of these elemental laws. There is only the way of intuition, which is helped by a feeling for the order lying behind the appearance."

— ALBERT EINSTEIN

SHARE YOUR TRUTH AND MAKE A DIFFERENCE

"Our greatness lies not so much in being able to remake the world, but in being able to remake ourselves."

— MAHATMA GANDHI

Earlier in this book, I mentioned that the five-step journey to becoming successful, having beautiful relationships, and being at peace with yourself is based on generations of knowledge. The greatest masters in modern history—including Mahatma Gandhi, Albert Einstein, and Mother Teresa—not only made life-changing discoveries that enabled them to overcome great personal challenges; they also made it their mission to share their knowledge with the world and empower others to see and process life in a more positive light.

Mother Teresa is an excellent example of the value of seeing life as it is—full of possibilities. She believed in approaching people with an open mind, in order to avoid judging them and to truly love them. She consistently harnessed the power of positive energy through kind words with "endless echoes." She believed in doing things with all her heart and soul and invited others to "do small things with great love."

Her mission didn't end with the kind deeds she performed. She also sought to spark a mental, emotional, and spiritual transformation... one that would propel everyday people to see the beauty of giving to others and of sharing the wisdom and resources they were lucky enough to come by.

You, too, have your own story to share. By this stage of your reading, you have seen the power that lies in deciding where you are and where you want to be. You also know that conditioning your mind for the win is vital if you are to achieve your goals, and that relying on a smart plan can help keep you on track.

If this book has inspired you to create greater abundance, build happy relationships, and find your own inner calm in the storm, know that you can help someone who is struggling to find purpose and commit to a winning plan.

By leaving a review of this book on Amazon, you'll show other readers where they can find a master method that will transform their lives and help them achieve all their professional and personal goals.

Simply by letting other readers know how this book has helped you and what they'll find inside, you'll help them find the guidance that will set them on a positive course of discovery and change.

Thank you so much for your support. As a truth seeker, you know the great value of sharing the pillars of success. Through your generosity, you attract the kind of positive energy that serves to propel you even further in your quest for meaning and success.

Scan the QR code below!

STEP 3: PLAN

DESIGNING YOUR PERSONAL WINNING PLAN OF ACTION

PLANNING FOR SUCCESS

You're well on your way to a wonderful life, now that you've chosen your destination (Step1: **Defining What You Want**) and you're actively and consciously working on achieving your most healthy, positive frame of mind possible (Step 2: **Conditioning Your Mind**) for the journey and beyond. Now you're ready to actually lay out a plan with action steps that will enable you to materialize your desires with Step 3 of The Master Method - **Designing Your Winning Plan of Action**.

This is where the excitement REALLY begins! You have your goal already in your mind. You've written it down. You've read it. You've re-read it. You've pictured it and visualized it in every way. Now let's move forward toward your destination by creating a winning PLAN so you will have a clear and detailed road map to follow.

Make a Plan and Commit to It

When I was a teenager, I got up very early in the morning and I did 180 pushups, 180 sit-ups, 180 squats, and 1,000 kicks faithfully every day before school. I never missed a day. A few years ago, I ran into someone I dated in my early days of training. In that conversation, she reminded me that I always kept her waiting before we went out. I had a set workout that was part of my plan to become a world champion and nothing — not even a fun date — could keep me from my disciplined training routine. If I set 180 pushups as my goal, then I did 180 pushups, not 100 …or 150 … or even 179! I had my plan and I stuck to it, no matter what.

"The power of intuitive understanding will protect you from harm until the end of your days."

— LAO TZU

CHARTING YOUR ROUTE

Once you know without a doubt what your destination is AND you're working on conditioning your mind to keep you in the strongest, most positive and best "mind shape" possible, you'll need a detailed roadmap to get you there. So begin by outlining your plan. If you skip this important step, you could end up wasting time and energy haphazardly going down paths that will only delay your success. Your roadmap plan will detail your steps and allow you to take the most efficient and timely route to your endpoint. Once you've mapped out your plan, your positive thoughts, feelings, and energy will be directed and will work most efficiently in creating opportunities and experiences that will enable you to achieve your success.

Why Make a Plan?

Imagine you lived in Buffalo, New York, and decide to take a road trip to Los Angeles, California. You're excited about going to LA, anticipating the smell of the ocean and the 80-degree warmth, and you're looking forward to being on the West Coast very soon. You could just hop in your car with no GPS or map, guess which way is west, and start driving. At each cross-road, you would guess which direction to turn, only to discover it's wrong, delaying your journey. You're not sure where you are or how to get where you're going, and soon you feel as though you've been driving around aimlessly and gotten nowhere.

Taking a trip this way would create endless frustration (not to mention waste a lot of time AND gas), and because you have no direction and have been driving around in circles making no progress, you may even give up and decide not to make the trip at all. You knew where you wanted to go, but you had no plan of *how* to get there.

On the other hand, carefully planning your route and having a map before you begin your journey would make this trip much more enjoyable, and you would arrive at your destination more quickly. You wouldn't be worried along the way, since you planned it ahead of time, and you could even enjoy the scenery, feeling relaxed and looking forward to your arrival. Even if you run into unexpected roadblocks, detours, traffic, or bad weather that weren't part of the original plan... as long as you keep your destination in mind ... AND your plan allows for minor detours, you can make adjustments. In the end, you might even find yourself on a better road.

"Create a definite plan for carrying out your desire and begin at once, whether you are ready or not, to put this plan into action."

— NAPOLEON HILL

Build in Flexibility

The purpose of developing your roadmap is to determine and outline specifically what you need to do to accomplish your goal. These are the exact steps you'll take to get to your final destination. Even though you're creating a detailed plan, always allow for unexpected challenges and detours, and be prepared to revise steps as necessary. As long as you take consistent action and maintain the faith that challenges are meant to provide you with the tools you need to keep moving forward, you WILL continue to move forward! Plan well, take action, but always be flexible.

Once you've outlined your plan, remember it's not definite, rigid or set in stone. It's meant to be a simple, MODIFIABLE guideline to help you take action steps, enabling you to go after your goal one piece at a time. You must be able to adjust your plan and adapt it when you realize one of the steps may not be working, or if it's taking you in the wrong direction.

If you reach a point where you're not sure about how to adjust your plan or which path to take, don't panic. Take a pause, relax, breathe, watch, and listen. Trust your intuition and have faith that the answers will come. Sometimes that pause is a needed break to reassess, re-energize, and clear your mind to see things from different angles. Try to be receptive and open to the answers, solutions, or opportunities whenever and however they are shown to you. Don't be concerned about when and how it will happen. Just have faith that the right path will be presented to you at the right moment.

If things don't feel right, trust the feeling. Then be receptive to the other opportunities that are waiting for you to notice them. Be actively open to receiving your answers. The right path will FEEL right. Sit back and relax for a moment, or perhaps for a few days or even a few weeks. Open your mind, research options, and observe people, situations, and possibilities around you. Be patient, and have unwavering faith that the right path will be shown to you. And when it's shown to you and it feels right — TAKE ACTION!

Bumps in the Road Make You Stronger

On your journey to success, remember the people and experiences you encounter along the way are giving you the tools, strength, and character to complete the rest of your journey. No experience or encounter is a waste of time. You'll always benefit from each person you meet and from each experience, even if it initially feels like a tough challenge.

For example, difficult people and problematic experiences teach us patience, compassion, and perseverance. Accept every individual and experience you encounter with gratitude, because you're becoming a stronger, wiser, more patient person as a result. These experiences are preparing you for the next step in achieving your goal and future goals. Don't be discouraged, and keep your eye on your destination. Move forward through the difficulties, over the bumps in the road, and around the roadblocks, because once you come out on the other side, you'll understand how much stronger you are. You'll find yourself even closer to the life of your dreams, as long as you continue to move forward positively.

Visual Reminders

You already know what you want, and you've written it down. Now, write it again, and say it out loud! Say it as if you already have it, and express how you feel about it. For example, "I am so happy I started my own business and I'm financially free!" Write it on a piece of paper and tape it to your mirror. Put another one in your wallet, on your desk, and in your car. In fact, put this book down, write it, and say it out loud right now!

The more you remind yourself of your destination, the more you'll keep yourself in the right frame of mind, and this will keep you moving forward.

ONE STEP AT A TIME

Now it's time to clearly determine the exact steps necessary to get where you're going. Start by writing down an outline of objectives that need to be accomplished in order to achieve your goal. Under each objective, gradually detail the sub-steps, until you have a very clear detailed strategy. Then break these sub-steps down even further into daily or weekly To-Do lists. Every objective can be defined as a small goal in itself, leading you to your larger goal. As you accomplish each step, be sure to celebrate each one!

Defining incremental steps allows you to focus on small short-term goals one at a time. Oftentimes if a goal is too large, it seems unattainable because it feels so far away. You may find yourself getting lost, discouraged, or impatient and you may even give up because the big goal seems so far off. However, if you divide the large goal into smaller sub-goals, you'll feel accomplished along the way, and eventually, you'll reach the larger goal in a much more efficient manner.

In martial arts, earning a black belt is a journey. The first step is to learn the most basic techniques to earn your first belt. After earning that belt, the focus is shifted toward the next set of techniques to earn the next belt. Each belt level consists of its own list of requirements to achieve that belt. Each belt is celebrated as its own accomplishment, but all the while, the student is keeping the final goal in mind — the black belt.

Similarly, if you wish to become a doctor, there are specific steps, such as pre-med classes, the MCAT exam, and gaining a certain amount of practical experience in order to be accepted to medical school, and each of these steps is a small goal in itself. Once in medical school, each class may also be considered a small sub-goal toward your ultimate goal of becoming a physician. You take each step incrementally, earning your small achievements, but always keeping in mind and visualizing what you're ultimately working toward. You actually SEE yourself achieving it and you feel the excitement NOW.

Little Steps Add Up to Big Accomplishments

No matter what you hope to achieve — losing weight, earning a certain amount of money, or improving a relationship — outlining your plan to reach your goal is vital to getting there most efficiently. Breaking your large goal down into smaller goals allows for the achievement of small victories that will make you feel successful along the way. These victories will motivate you to work even harder and more enthusiastically toward the next step. Eventually, each step will be accomplished, and your final destination will be reached!

This concept will be repeated over and over again because it's so vital: Always keep your goal in mind. Even while you're taking the little steps and celebrating your incremental achievements, never lose sight of the final destination. It's an important skill to be able to zoom in and out constantly, being able to take care of your daily tasks, while remembering what you're ultimately working to achieve.

Keep Your Eyes on the Prize

Sometimes it's possible to get so immersed in the smaller steps that you forget where you're going. It's far too easy to get stuck in the process and never reach your endpoint. You may get too comfortable where you are and lose your drive, or get discouraged that it's not happening fast enough.

Keeping your final goal in mind will help in overcoming unexpected circumstances that may frustrate you or challenge your motivation to keep going. Sometimes the "clutter" from the past we spoke of earlier begins to accumulate in our minds again, especially if we're faced with challenges. We allow fear or unworthiness or doubt to affect our thoughts and actions, or we reach a point where we don't want to leave our comfort zone physically, mentally, or emotionally. It's at these moments when you must really rely on your faith in the universe, have patience, and remember your path WILL take you where you want to go. You'll reach your destination, as long as you stay positive, feel good, and KEEP TAKING ACTION. You will keep going and will find the way. Constantly remind yourself of the wonderful end result you're working to achieve, and continue the forward momentum with patience and faith.

Immerse yourself in activities and spend time with people who make you feel good, align with your intentions, and share your positive energy. It's also really powerful to surround yourself with like-minded people with common goals, who may be on a similar journey. They can provide you with inspiration, encouragement, and ideas, because of their similar interests.

Go back to the Feel Good list you made in Step 1 and use it to re-energize your positive mindset. Read books that make you feel good that can enlighten you with helpful knowledge. Watch programs that make you happy. Exercise and stay active so your body feels healthy. Surround yourself with what makes you feel peaceful and happy because all of these good feelings will create incredibly powerful energy to keep you on track. Here's a reminder of some great feel-good fixers:

- Go for a walk or exercise
- Meditate
- Spend time with positive people who make you feel happy
- Watch a funny movie
- Play your favorite sport
- Listen to music that lifts your spirits
- Experience the sights and sounds of nature
- Spend time with a beloved pet
- Go to the bookstore and browse through feel-good books and music
- Have a favorite delicious (and healthy) meal

- READ THIS BOOK AGAIN!
- Do what makes you smile, laugh and feel joyful
- Do what brings you peace

PUT YOUR PLAN INTO GEAR

Now that you've learned how to map out your plan, it's time to take action! Get started right away, while everything is fresh in your mind. Use this next exercise to get your ideas out of your head and onto paper. Once you begin, you'll be inspired, and you'll have your roadmap and To Do lists. You'll be empowered to take action and check your boxes, focusing on one small step at a time.

So "stay in the car," no matter what twists and turns may lie ahead…keep driving forward, and before you know it, you'll arrive at the destination of your dreams. Once you know The Master Method and put all of its steps into practice, you'll have the system, the tools, the wisdom, and the strength to accomplish so many different things, in every area of your life.

EXERCISE: CHECKLIST OF STEPS

In your journal, write down at least five steps necessary for the attainment of your goals in each of the five areas of your life: Career, Finances, Relationships, Health, and Inner Peace.

Give yourself a timeline or goal dates to complete each step and indicate it clearly.

Then make daily checklists of action items to accomplish toward those steps, and with each task you check off, allow yourself to feel a sense of advancement and satisfaction that you're moving closer and closer to your ultimate goal.

Keep in mind, you may add and modify steps along the way. If something isn't working, revise your plan accordingly. Plan well, but allow for flexibility.

And to make it even more fun, work in some mini-rewards for yourself as you accomplish your milestones. For example, anytime you reach a milestone, you can celebrate with a special meal, outing, or day off to relax. This can keep the process inspiring for you along the way to your final destination.

Just keep going - you can do this!

CAREER		FINANCES		RELATIONSHIPS	
Step	Date	Step	Date	Step	Date
1. a. b. c.	1. a. b. c.	1. a. b. c.	1. a. b. c.	1. a. b. c.	1. a. b. c.
2. a. b. c.	2. a. b. c.	2. a. b. c.	2. a. b. c.	2. a. b. c.	2. a. b. c.

HEALTH		INNER PEACE	
Step	Date	Step	Date
1. a. b. c.	1. a. b. c.	1. a. b. c.	1. a. b. c.
2. a. b. c.	2. a. b. c.	2. a. b. c.	2. a. b. c.

STEP 4: CREATE

TAKING ACTION & CREATING THE LIFE YOU DESERVE

Congratulations on completing Step 3 of The Master Method! In this step, you designed a winning plan with detailed steps to achieve your ultimate goals. With a winning plan now in place, it's time to activate each of the steps and make your vision a reality. In Step 4 you will now be taking consistent action and actively create the life you truly deserve.

JUST START

Starting your personal growth journey can be daunting. It's easy to feel overwhelmed by the sheer magnitude of what needs to be done. But the truth is that the secret to personal growth lies in taking the first step. Don't procrastinate, or wait till conditions are perfect before you begin. Start where you are, take what you have, and move forward.

It's natural to feel the need to create a perfect plan before taking any steps. But overthinking can lead to paralysis. Before you know it, days turn into weeks, months into years, and you're still standing at the starting line. Recognize that perfection is unattainable and that your plan doesn't have to be flawless. Identify the steps that make sense to you and take action consistently.

As you start this journey, don't forget that progress comes in many forms. Small steps taken consistently can lead to great results. The key is consistently working towards your goals. Understand that personal growth is a process of trial and error. You will make mistakes, face setbacks and encounter challenges, but every experience is an opportunity for growth.

Remember that personal growth is a journey. And it is part of the process. Allow yourself to enjoy the process, take pride in your accomplishments, and appreciate how far you've come. By moving forward on your journey today and every day, you are taking steps toward becoming the best version of yourself.

THE EVERYDAY RULE

The Everyday Rule is a powerful tool for achieving success in life. It is a simple philosophy that encourages us to make the most of every day by taking action toward our goals. By following this rule, we can avoid procrastination, eliminate distractions and stay focused on what matters most–achieving our ultimate goals and creating a life of abundance, happiness, and peace.

To make the most of the Everyday Rule, follow these helpful tips.

- Set incremental goals. When we set goals that are too big or too daunting, we can become overwhelmed and lose motivation. By breaking goals down into smaller, more manageable steps, you'll make progress every day and build momentum toward your ultimate objective.
- Plan your day the night before. This is a valuable habit to cultivate. By setting goals and tasks for the day ahead, we can hit the ground running in the morning and avoid wasting time on indecision or procrastination.
- Eliminate distractions. Turning off our phones during productive times or finding a quiet place to work, can help us stay focused and avoid getting sidetracked.
- Schedule your day. Schedule your pockets of productive time by detailing the tasks for the day, and even schedule in your breaks. Taking breaks is also important for maintaining productivity and motivation. Trying to work for extended periods without rest can lead to burnout and a loss of enthusiasm. By taking regular breaks and stepping away from our work, we can recharge and come back to the task at hand with renewed energy and focus.
- Reward yourself! When we reward ourselves for completing important tasks it is a powerful motivator. Celebrating your accomplishments, no matter how small, will give you a sense of accomplishment and help you stay positive and motivated.

Following the Everyday Rule will help you stay focused, motivated, and on track toward your goals. It may not be easy, but the rewards are worth it. By taking action every day, you will build the habits and mindset of success, and achieving your ultimate objectives will be inevitable!

ANALYZE PROGRESS, MAKE ADJUSTMENTS, AND KEEP MOVING!

As you move forward on your journey to your goals and aspirations, it's crucial to regularly evaluate your progress and make adjustments as necessary. As much as it's important to stay consistent, it's equally important to analyze the effectiveness of your actions and adapt your strategies accordingly.

If you come across a situation where you feel like what you're doing isn't working out, take a moment to pause, evaluate the situation, and brainstorm alternative courses of action. This can help you stay on track and make sure that you are progressing in the right direction.

It's natural to encounter bumps and roadblocks along the way, but it's important to receive them with the best attitude, staying flexible and open to making changes. Don't be afraid to abandon a strategy or idea if it's not working out – your ultimate success depends on your willingness to adapt and pivot.

REMEMBER TO CELEBRATE!

It's so important to celebrate your successes, no matter how small or seemingly insignificant they might be. Every win, no matter how big or small, deserves recognition and positivity. Celebrating your small accomplishments will help you maintain your motivation and keep moving forward.

The best plan is the one that you take action on. So don't wait around for things to happen – make a plan, take action, evaluate, adjust, and keep moving forward! You're on your way, and you're in control now!

STEP 5: ENDURE

STAYING ON TRACK THROUGH THE BUMPS

Congratulations! You've reached the last step of The Master Method in *The Mindset Guide for Winners!*

Let's quickly review The Master Method steps so far:

Step 1: Define What You Want

You began by deciding what you want. You started a journal, where you acknowledged what you don't want and listed what you do want. You assessed your starting point and learned about the power of thought and the thought-feelings-energy connection. You learned about choosing the positive path and began thinking about your goals in the five areas of life: Career, Finances, Relationships, Health and Inner Peace. Here you learned that you are the creator of your own reality.

Step 2: Condition Your Mind

In this chapter, you discovered the importance of conditioning your mind for success through five essential elements: Gratitude, Humility, Positivity, Faith, and Patience. You learned that you can actually redirect and change your thinking, that losing is nothing more than a part of winning, and that it's possible to reset your default for positivity. You were also given some techniques for overcoming roadblocks and dealing with difficult people, as well as sustaining your faith and practicing patience.

Step 3: Design Your Plan

Now we got down to the importance of preparing a roadmap and sticking to it, with the knowledge that attaining your large goals will be faster when you create smaller incremental goals and build flexibility into your plan.

Step 4: Take Action and Create Your Life!

Implementing your plan with intentional consistent action is the key to Step 4. You are in creation mode, and you are actively and consistently moving forward!

In this last Step 5, we'll discuss some final strategies and vital elements that will help you stay on track when you face challenges, adversity, and difficult times.

Embarking on a journey to greatness is never a smooth, straight path - there are twists and turns, bumps and hurdles that will undoubtedly have the ability to stunt your progress. Yet, it's essential to keep in mind that these challenges are simply a part of the process, and they don't have the power to keep us from reaching our goals. In fact, it's those who continuously fight through adversity that go on to see their dreams come to fruition. It's those who proactively move forward with the intention of overcoming every challenge, are the ones who will reach their destination of success.

Don't let the fear of overcoming obstacles hold you back. Though it may feel impossible to push through during difficult times, know that you have the strength within you to conquer all. But, it's critical that you remain intentional with your actions, consistent with your efforts, and you're always aware of what's next in your plan.

Attaining the success that you so deeply desire is not just a possibility– it's entirely, positively, and absolutely attainable. Believe in your potential and in your power, and work towards it fearlessly. You've got what it takes!

SELF-DISCIPLINE AND STRENGTH OF MIND

When I decided at the age of 15 to become a kickboxing world champion, I knew it wasn't going to happen overnight. I knew it would require a huge amount of conditioning and the development of techniques. I knew I needed experience to understand the mechanics of fighting, and the work required would be extremely difficult. BUT I also knew, without a doubt, where I wanted to be, and I knew I would do whatever it took to get there.

In order to fight at a world championship level, a large part of my plan was not just to get into shape, but also to work until I had the best-conditioned lightweight class body in the world. In order to do that, I had to get up early EVERY SINGLE DAY and do the work required to carry out my plan. And that took self-discipline.

But how exactly do you develop the discipline you need once you've started work on your plan?

Self-discipline is an important aspect of life that plays a vital role in ensuring success and achievement in any field. It involves the ability to control your thoughts and actions and to do what needs to be done every day to achieve your ultimate goal. It's not just about motivation, but about consistency, persistence, and focus.

Self-Discipline is a Process in Itself

To begin with, developing self-discipline starts with a burning desire - a desire that fills you with excitement, positive energy, and a sense of anticipation. Without this burning desire, it will be challenging to maintain the discipline required to keep going when things get tough.

You must keep your eyes on the end goal, reminding yourself constantly of what you are going to achieve. This helps you to focus your energies, stay motivated and keep moving forward throughout the process.

Proactively keeping a positive attitude is also critical when it comes to self-discipline. Your state of mind has a significant impact on the success or failure of your efforts. If you wake up every morning, complaining about all the things on your list, dreading the day ahead, you're setting yourself up for a difficult day. However, if you choose to start your day with a positive outlook, gratitude, and focusing on your accomplishments instead of your challenges, you'll find that the day flows more smoothly and you're better able to complete your tasks.

To improve and expand your self-discipline, you need to think creatively. For instance, we discussed the process of breaking down your goal into smaller, more achievable tasks, setting deadlines for each task, and rewarding yourself for completing each milestone. Alternatively, you can find a coach or account-ability partner to keep you on track, practice visualizations and meditations to see yourself succeeding and eliminate any distractions or negative influences that might derail your progress.

At this point, self-discipline becomes your ability to do what you need to do, when you need to do it, no matter what. No excuses. No rationalizations for why you aren't going to get it done, or why it can wait. No procrastinating or giving up on a task. Your self-discipline will drive you to diligently and persis-tently get things done. You'll have the mindset of not being satisfied until the task at hand is complete and the box is checked. You will also have the mindset to keep moving forward, finding solutions when you experience challenges, and looking at setbacks as lessons, not reasons to stop.

Self-discipline is a process that requires that burning desire deep within you, focus, consistency, and a positive attitude. It's essential to maintain these qualities and remain motivated throughout the journey, so you can overcome any obstacle that comes your way.

When you master the art of self-discipline, you'll find that you'll have an extra superpower to achieve anything you set your mind to, regardless of your current circumstances or if you experience unexpected challenges along the way.

ENTHUSIASM

The secret to achieving your goals lies not only in the amount of effort you put in, but also in the spirit with which you approach your tasks. As the great success guru Napoleon Hill once said, "There are no shortcuts to great achievements."

You must commit to working hard, and doing so with enthusiasm is the key to unlocking your full potential. Every little bit of effort that you put into your work counts towards your success. If you approach your tasks with a negative attitude or without feeling good about them, it will show in your results. In fact, you might not see any results at all.

To achieve your goals, you must have the self-discipline to perform your tasks to the very best of your ability. And just as importantly, you need to commit to your plans with enthusiasm and passion. This combination of hard work and creativity will take you far, and help you to achieve success beyond your wildest dreams. Remember: with the right attitude, anything is possible.

CHAMPIONSHIP TRAINING

For many years, my training routine in preparation for competitions was to start each day, with 45 minutes of running. This was only a fraction of my training and it was just the beginning of my morning. Following my 45-minute run (which also included sprinting and jumping) I would head to the boxing gym for 3 hours to work my hands on the speed bag, heavy bag and pads, and also work on reaction time drills and sparring. From the boxing gym, it was time to teach martial arts classes until 9 pm, after which I would begin the third section of my training in the late evening. For 2 hours, I worked on kicking and leg conditioning with kicking pads, sparring with my feet, speed drills, and endurance drills. I finished my training at about 11:00 pm, and by the time I got home, I was absolutely exhausted and oftentimes beat up. But I knew this work was necessary because I wanted to become the best!

The next morning, the routine started all over again. Now, to get up and follow this training program for a day or two is one thing. However, to diligently and consistently carry out these instructions every single day for months and months is completely different. Often, I was so physically spent, with aching muscles and, on occasion, injuries. I would look ahead, and see the day in front of me just the same as the day before and the day before. Regardless of the schedule, regardless of the weather, and regardless of the pain I was feeling, I still had to get up every morning to train … and sometimes my mind and body made it unbelievably difficult.

"However many holy words you read, however many you speak, what good would it do if you don't act upon them."

— BUDDHA

IT'S ALL ABOUT ATTITUDE

What I learned throughout those years is that it was my CHOICE to either get up and hate what I was doing, or do it knowing this was getting me closer to becoming a world champion. As I lay there early in the morning, especially when I was tired and beat up, I would consciously remind myself what I wanted to accomplish, and I would visualize the end result. I took myself to that place in my mind, victorious, feeling the joy, hearing the cheers from the crowd, and feeling the rush of happiness and pride at that moment of reaching my destination.

I would also remind myself of what I was grateful for - my health, family, and friends, and I would actively bring myself into a positive mindset. I was able to consciously and intentionally feel good about what I needed to accomplish that day, and so I would get up, and literally say to myself out loud, "This is going to be a GREAT DAY." I thought about how much I was going to improve because of my training. I KNEW the world championship was already on its way, and I felt happy and excited. This excitement gave me the motivation and energy not only to get up but to get up with enthusiasm to attack my tasks.

I felt happy to be improving, regardless if it was 17 degrees or if there was snow and ice on the ground. I was happy to be that much closer to my goal and this positive mental attitude took me down the path to become a world champion, not just once but seven times.

BREAKING THE BARRIERS

Sometimes your unconditioned mind will take over and try and trick you into doing things the easy way, such as putting things off until tomorrow or telling you, "I know you're tired. You should just rest today and then do better tomorrow." Or your mind may even try and tell you, "This isn't worth the effort. Maybe you should just stop now. Just give up. Then you can relax!"

Cultivating a winning mindset means actively pushing past negative thoughts that can cause roadblocks in our path to success. These barriers often stem from deep-seated emotions, but it's important to realize that regardless of their origin, it's up to us to decide whether we let them hold us back.

It may feel daunting, but with a bit of determination, anyone can overcome these obstacles. Here are some tips to help you along the way:

- Recognize and acknowledge your negative thoughts/feelings when they appear, but don't let them consume you.
- Imagine those feelings (doubt, worry, fear, unworthiness, etc) passing right through you and leaving you.
- Shift your focus to positive thoughts. Remember your strengths and past successes. Turn negative thoughts and feelings around by focusing on gratitude and things that bring you joy.
- DO things that make you feel good

- Remind yourself that you ARE worthy, you don't need to fear and you are capable
- Choose to not allow others to disrupt the strong positive feelings you've worked so hard to attain
- Surround yourself with supportive people who believe in you and your abilities.

AN HONEST LOOK INSIDE

One of the conversations I had with one of my wisest teachers, the Tibetan Lama Tinku Nyima Rinpoche, was a life-changing moment for me. One evening as I visited him in his private chamber, he was explaining to me the importance of self-discipline in order to carry one's life in a positive way, and avoiding negative thoughts and negative actions.

As I listened to these teachings, overwhelming feelings of repentance washed over me and I felt terrible as images of mistakes I had made and regretful things I had done in my past came to my mind. I shared with him so many of these feelings I was experiencing at that moment, and as he listened, he simply smiled, and he said, "Good."

Puzzled, I asked my teacher, "Why do you refer to these feelings I'm having as 'good'?" He smiled again and gently explained, "Because now, you know what you don't want to be."

To remain positive, you must first understand the root of your thoughts/feelings, determine where they truly originate, and ask yourself if those feelings have a positive purpose. For example, if you're angry, is being angry going to solve your problem?

Will it serve a positive purpose? It would be much better to let those feelings pass through you and transform your energy into finding solutions. Positive solutions.

Your ego will find any excuse to justify and place blame on others for your negative thoughts, feelings, and actions ("I am really angry because of HIS behavior," or "I'm not going to help her because she was rude."). Learn to become the master of your own thoughts and emotions and actions, and proactively replace negative emotions with positive solution-based thoughts. YOU control your emotions and what you allow yourself to feel about a person or a situation.

Taking responsibility for our emotions is crucial to maintaining a healthy state of mind. Blaming others or outside circumstances only perpetuates negative feelings. To develop self-discipline and truly understand our emotions, it's important to be honest with ourselves.

Here are some questions to ask yourself when faced with negative emotions:

- What am I feeling right now? Anger? Jealousy? Annoyance? Frustration?
- Am I blaming someone or outside circumstances for this feeling?
- Why do I feel this way? What is the root of this feeling?
- Am I fearful of losing control? Discomfort? Pain? Losing someone? Abandonment?
- Is this emotion helping me? Will it change the situation or make it any better?

- How can I look at the situation objectively and observe it without emotion?
- How can I turn this around in a positive way?

Answering these questions can help you become more self-aware and better equipped to intentionally handle negative emotions. Remember, we are 100% responsible for our emotions and resulting behaviors, and we have the power to change the outcome by changing our mindset. Taking control of your emotions will lead you to more positive actions, inter-actions, circumstances, and opportunities and ultimately to a happier, more fulfilling life.

SHIFTING FROM NEGATIVE TO POSITIVE

Monitoring thoughts and shifting them to maintain a positive frame of mind is one of the most difficult things for any human being to master. Sometimes it seems impossible to find that positive seed, especially when everything feels like it's going wrong around you. You're overwhelmed, frustrated, discour-aged and you feel as though you're failing. This is when you need to stop and give yourself a break.

You're certainly not alone in experiencing these feelings. You are human! Maybe you're tired. Allow yourself rest. Take some time to back away from the frustration and the discouragement and just let yourself breathe very peacefully for a moment.

Close your eyes, and breathe very slowly in through your nose, and out through your mouth. Consciously relax each muscle in your body from the top of your head down to the tips of your toes. Feel yourself becoming more and more relaxed, and imagine all of the frustration leaving your body and being replaced with light, peace, and calm. Allow yourself this moment, enjoy this feeling, and sit with it peacefully and quietly for a little while.

Once you've restored a sense of peace and calm within you, now restore that picture in your mind of the goal you are striving for. Don't think about your day, obstacles, challenges, or your frustrations. Think of your destination. Picture it, know you will be there, enjoy it, and shift your feelings back to a positive vibrational state.

Helpful thoughts and reminders for shifting gears:

- This experience is strengthening me.
- This experience is providing me with valuable tools I will need later.
- This experience is giving me wisdom I will need later.
- This experience is showing me contrast, so I will really appreciate the other extreme - the joy of overcoming this obstacle.
- This experience is only temporary.
- The faster I can shift my energy back to positive, the faster I will be back on track, and on the right path to my goal.
- Giving this situation positive energy rather than responding negatively will result in a faster resolution.

Once you can truly understand this power and the nature of your thought, you're able to master controlling your vibrational energy. You become the master of your mind. Understanding your thoughts will improve your outlook, any circumstance, experience, and your relationships with everyone you encounter.

The road to success may not be easy, but with a positive mindset and a refusal to let negative thoughts hold you back, it's achievable. Keep pushing forward and believe in yourself. You've got this!

EXERCISE: REVIEW THE DAY

Every day, try to find a quiet moment. Close your eyes. Relax your body. Visualize your muscles beginning to relax. When you introduce yourself to the relaxation state, let thoughts come into your mind. Don't repress them. Let them come, then let them go. Let them in, then let them out. Empty your mind.

Now replay your day, beginning with the last encounter with the last person in your day. What did you do? What did you say? What was the interaction? Don't identify yourself with the situation. If it was happy, don't get happy. If it was sad, don't get sad. Look at it in the third person, very objectively. If something made you angry in the moment, in this replay observe it intentionally without feeling emotion. Just look at it ... and move on to the next scene. Watch it like a movie. Move on to the situation before that, and the one before that, and the one before that, until you see yourself waking up that morning.

You've now gone through the whole day of experiences and you've replayed everything you encountered — without the emotion. You're now able to have a different view of your day, and this helps to remove the negativity that may have resulted from your experiences. You've shifted yourself to a positive frame of mind, which will keep you on the right path of doing what you need to do — completing your tasks and carrying out your plan for success.

FINAL THOUGHTS, TIPS & REMINDERS

C ONGRATULATIONS!

If you've gotten to this point, you were truly meant to receive everything you've read in *The Mindset Guide for Winners - 5 Steps to Become a Champion in Your Life.*

I sincerely hope you/ve been inspired by the steps of "The Master Method" and feel you have gained the tools and the confidence to follow your innermost dreams. I truly believe you will achieve everything you set your intentions toward, if you diligently, consistently, and enthusiastically follow the Master Method steps.

Here are a few final reminders and tips to inspire, motivate & keep you on track:

1 — Remember: YOU ARE WORTHY.

Don't let the voices of your past tell you you won't succeed. Free your mind from those voices. You were created pure and perfect—that's the true essence of who you are. Your only job is to go back and reconnect with that source of purity, and your highest self. The incredible life you truly desire is yours! The trick is: you must believe you deserve it. When you decide to acknowledge that YOU ARE WORTHY, YOU ARE CAPABLE, and YOU TRULY DESERVE the life you desire, you will open the gates for a successful life filled with abundance.

2 — Your power is unlimited.

Don't feel powerless, allowing yourself to become a victim of circumstances. Within you is everything you need to CREATE the life you truly want. That universal force that drives every-thing and everyone — the source, infinite intelligence, supreme power, or however you choose to accept it — is present in everyone and everything. When you remain conscious of this force and your connection to it, your power to create is unlimited!

3 — Don't let fear rule your life.

Fear is one of the leading causes of negative thinking and fail-ure. There are many types of fears that can influence our minds — fear of rejection, fear of failure, fear of embarrassment, fear of poverty, fear of losing the ones you love, fear of "what are they going to say," fear of sickness, fear of death. No matter what kind of fear lives within you, it only holds you back and prevents the expansion of your mind, body, and spirit.

For any fear you may experience, empower yourself to eradicate them with visualizations, positive affirmations, and a plan to walk through the fear, pass it by, and leave it behind you. Tell yourself, "If my friends reject me, I'll find new friends who will support me. If I fail, I'll learn a valuable lesson to help me reach my goal. It doesn't matter what others think about me. Their opinions don't matter and will not diminish what I think of myself or change my focus. If someone I love decides to walk on a different path, my thoughts will be with them, and I will wish them a safe and successful journey." Once again, as long as you focus on what you want and positively shift your thoughts, everything you experience benefits you and will bring you closer to your goal.

4 — Fill yourself with love and compassion.

Love is the most powerful of all emotions. It will help you see the best in everyone and appreciate the world around you. It allows you to bypass external layers of personality, see everyone on a deeper level, and find connections with all beings. Love allows you to see beyond the surface, developing understanding and patience as a result.

Compassion is the antidote for anger and many other negative emotions. We can feel compassion if we try to understand others and look beyond negative behavior and attempt to understand where the root of their negativity is coming from. It may be a lack of knowledge or their own fears and insecurities.

Understanding this will help you to see them in a different light.

5 — Find joy in everything that surrounds you.

We are not just in this universe, but we are a part of it. Allow yourself to be in the present in each moment. Feel the wind. Listen to the birds. Feel the energy of the trees and the plants. Just enjoy being in the presence of what surrounds you. This awareness and appreciation will bring you a sense of great peace and tranquility. Always give yourself an opportunity to acknowledge, appreciate and enjoy your surroundings.

6 — Surround yourself with people who will support your frame of mind, and avoid people who are a negative influence.

"Enthusiasm is the yeast that makes your hopes shine to the stars. Enthusiasm is the sparkle in your eyes, the swing in your gait, the grip of your hand, the irresistible surge of will and energy to execute your ideas."

— HENRY FORD

Successful people surround themselves with other successful people. They feed off of each other's positive energy, empowering themselves through their interactions. Their positive energies, knowledge, and enthusiasm are wonderful things to share. In contrast, the doom and gloom of surrounding yourself with pessimistic people will have that kind of impact on you as well. Avoid as much as possible interactions with people who criticize or unintentionally put you down, thinking they're giving you their opinion to "help" you. Instead, share your ideas and surround yourself with people who support your frame of mind or with people from whom you can take proper constructive advice.

7 — Rest well, and create healthy habits.

Taking care of your body and creating healthy habits are essential to increase your overall productivity. Having enough rest will increase your level of energy, you'll perform better and have a better mental attitude. Similarly, proper nutrition will improve the level and quality of your productivity, creating an overall wellness within you that will allow you to vibrate positively. Excesses will always have a negative impact on your body, and therefore it will have an effect on the way you perform. Live a life of balance and enjoy the results!

8 — Relax.

Worrying is not going to make what you want arrive any faster. One of the things many people "like" to do when they encounter a challenge is to get extra worried about it. Getting into a worrying frenzy will not help you find a solution faster. So change the cycle, change your vibration, focus peacefully and excitedly on what you really want, and you'll begin to attract good things.

9 — Allow time to learn something new.

Always keep your mind open to knowledge. Learn by observing others, by observing nature and everything surrounding you. Learn from a book, audiobook, podcast, or video. Learn from a teacher and from each day you live. By constantly expanding your mind, you keep it conditioned to seek and accept knowledge. You will become more equipped to live better and gain a deeper understanding of life and yourself."

"To enjoy good health, to bring true happiness to one's family, to bring peace to all, one must first discipline and control one's own mind. If a man can control his mind, he can find a way to enlightenment, and all wisdom and virtue will naturally come to him."

— BUDDHA

10 — Visit a new place.

Once in a while, it feels great to visit a new place. It doesn't have to be far away, and it doesn't have to require much time. Eat at a new restaurant. Watch a new movie. Go for a walk. I am always trying to find new places to visit. I love the mountains or lakes, and when I don't have much time, I try to find a fun place to go with my family, even if it's just a short nature walk. It helps renew energies and will get you out of a routine you may be falling into. Sometimes people go about their days, day after day, on autopilot, doing what they're supposed to do, without any energy or enthusiasm. Experiencing new places, or breaking your routine occasionally, will help you stay excited and enthusiastic! It will refresh your spirit, and it's FUN!

11 — Repeat the following statements out loud each day and as often as possible.

- I am worthy of success
- I am the creator of my life
- I am in control of my thoughts and my emotions
- I have unlimited power to create the life I desire
- I am so grateful for everything I have
- With every breath I take, inner peace and happiness fills me
- I choose positivity in my thoughts, feelings, behaviors, and actions

12— Take Action

When you have defined what you want and detailed your plan, don't wait! TAKE CONSISTENT ACTION. Procrastination will kill any plan. You must be PROACTIVE, START NOW, and MOVE FORWARD every day! Put your plan into practice, even if it isn't perfect or exactly how you want it to be. For anything you haven't figured out, the "doing" will give you direction and quickly teach you, revealing what needs to be adjusted in your original plan. Just get started!

PASSING THE KNOWLEDGE

As you start planning your personal winning plan of action, taking action, and sticking to it even in the face of challenges, you will feel more empowered to be a beacon of light for others.

Simply by sharing your honest opinion about the 5-step method, you'll show new readers where they can find the guidance to start pursuing the life they always wanted.

IN UNDER 1 MINUTE
YOU CAN HELP OTHERS JUST LIKE YOU BY LEAVING A REVIEW!

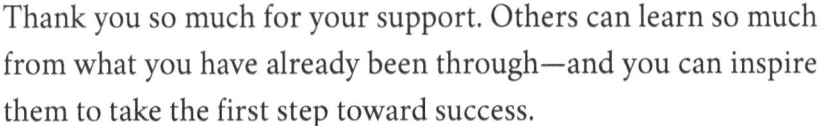

Thank you so much for your support. Others can learn so much from what you have already been through—and you can inspire them to take the first step toward success.

Scan the QR code below!

DREAM BIG!

In a world that often tells us to be realistic and settle for less, *The Mindset Guide for Winners* reminds us that anything is possible if you believe in yourself, maintain a positive frame of mind, and put in the work.

The 5-Step "Master Method" provides you with a roadmap for taking control of your life and achieving your dreams, and through the use of simple yet powerful exercises and visualizations, you have the power to condition your mind for success and cultivate a winning mindset of abundance and joy.

But this book is more than just a guide to achieving your goals. It is also a reminder to appreciate the journey, to find happiness in the present moment, to remember what you're grateful for, and to never give up on your dreams.

So, to all those who dare to dream big, may this book be your inspiration and guide, instilling in you the courage and determination to take that first step in creating the life you truly deserve. You are worthy, you are powerful, and YOU CAN DO THIS!

With gratitude and blessings,

The Master Method Academy &

Grandmaster Marco Sies

ABOUT THE AUTHORS

THE MASTER METHOD ACADEMY

The Master Method Academy provides educational offerings in leadership, martial arts, confidence-building, bully prevention, health, and wellness. Established in 2011, the academy focuses on positive education, fostering a positive mindset, and nurturing kindness, respect, and confidence. Academy staff members and educational contributors to the academy include professional educators and curriculum development specialists, educational psychologists, certified therapists and wellness coaches, and personal health & fitness coaches, in addition to their martial arts grandmasters, masters, and world champion coaches on staff.

Through its educational programs, community outreach, and publications, The Master Method Academy fosters the development of essential life skills that will profoundly impact personal growth and long-term success. Their programs address issues including bully prevention, conflict resolution, and positive mindset skill development, helping students develop tools to face challenges and achieve success with confidence and resilience.

The Master Method Academy goes beyond its educational offerings and actively engages with the local community and public schools through its Community Outreach Program. Their contributions include donations of equipment, supplies, education services, and funds to support schools and local initiatives. As a result, The Master Method Academy has garnered a strong relationship with its community through its educational and philanthropic endeavors.

GRANDMASTER MARCO SIES

Grandmaster Marco Sies is a 7-Time World Champion, 10th-degree grandmaster, educator, author, business owner, and television show host. Originally from Santiago, Chile, Grandmaster Marco started his martial arts training over 40 years ago, fought professionally for 14 years (kickboxing and boxing), and has been teaching professionally and donating his time to the community for more than 35 years.

Overcoming serious challenges including poverty, injury, and even homelessness, Grandmaster Marco used ancient and time-less universal principles to achieve his seven world champi-onships, nurture successful martial arts academies, publish educational materials, coach world champion athletes, and develop/advise businesses. He donates his time and resources to promote positive education, build community partnerships, and help educators, schools, and groups locally and internationally. Currently, he's producing a documentary series highlighting inspirational success stories while weaving in important social issues, mental health awareness, and providing resources for help, support, and education.

REFERENCES

100+ Inspiring Buddha Quotes on Life, Mediation, and Compassion. (2020). In Declutter the Mind. Retrieved from https://declutterthemind.com/blog/buddha-quotes/

Bargh, J. A., & Morsella, E. (2008). The unconscious mind. *Perspectives on psychological science: A journal of the Association for Psychological Science,* 3(1), 73.

Brainy Quote. (n.d.). *Mahatma Gandhi quotes.* https://www.brainyquote.com/quotes/mahatma_gandhi_163698

Gandhi, M., & Fischer, L. (Eds.). (2002). *The Essential Gandhi: An Anthology of His Writings on His Life, Work, and Ideas.* Vintage Spiritual Classics.

Gibran, K. (1923). *The Prophet.* Alfred A Knopf.

Henry Ford Quotations. (2023). In The Henry Ford. Retrieved from https://www.thehenryford.org

Hill, N. (2007). *Think and grow rich.* Jeremy P Tarcher.

Humility. (2021). In *Merriam-Webster Dictionary* (11th ed.). Retrieved from https://www.merriam-webster.com/

Humility. (2021). In *Oxford English Dictionary* (3rd ed.). Retrieved from https://www.oed.com/

James, W. (1907). The energies of men. *The Philosophical Review,* 16(1), 1-20.

Lao Tzu & Star, Jonathan. (2008). Tao Te Ching: The New Translation from Tao Te Ching, The Definitive Edition (Tarcher Cornerstone Editions). The Penguin Group.

Martial Development. (n.d.). From Homeless to World Champion: The Story of Kickboxer Marco Sies. Retrieved from https://www.martialdevelopment.com/world-champion-kickboxer-marco-sies/

Morukuru Family. (n.d.). *"Not all of us can do great things. But we can do small things with great love"* – Mother Teresa. https://morukuru.com/news/not-all-of-us-can-do-great-things-but-we-can-do-small-things-with-great-love-mother-teresa/

Origin of "I hear and I forget. I see and I remember. I do and I understand." (2016). In Stack Exchange. Retrieved from https://english.stackexchange.-

com/questions/226886/origin-of-i-hear-and-i-forget-i-see-and-i-remember-i-do-and-i-understand

Psychology Today. (2023, March 3). How Many Thoughts Are in Your Head? Psychology Today. Retrieved from https://www.psychologytoday.com/us/blog/get-out-of-your-mind/202303/how-many-thoughts-are-in-your-head

Thomas A. Edison Quotes. (2023). In AZ Quotes. Retrieved from https://www.azquotes.com/author/4358-Thomas_A_Edison

www.ingramcontent.com/pod-product-compliance
Lightning Source LLC
Chambersburg PA
CBHW031511120626
46545CB00005B/1837